M000283739

Accounts Payable
Best Practices

Accounts Payable
Best Practices

Mary S. Schaeffer

Executive Editor
IOMA's Report on Managing Accounts Payable

Co-creator
The Accounts Payable Certification Programs

WILEY

John Wiley & Sons, Inc.

This book is printed on acid-free paper. ∞

Copyright © 2004 by Mary S. Schaeffer and the Institute of Management and Administration, New York, NY. All rights reserved.

Published by John Wiley & Sons, Inc., Hoboken, New Jersey

Published simultaneously in Canada

No part of this publication may be reproduced, stored in a retrieval system, or transmitted in any form or by any means, electronic, mechanical, photocopying, recording, scanning, or otherwise, except as permitted under Section 107 or 108 of the 1976 United States Copyright Act, without either the prior written permission of the Publisher, or authorization through payment of the appropriate per-copy fee to the Copyright Clearance Center, Inc., 222 Rosewood Drive, Danvers, MA 01923, 978-750-8400, fax 978-646-8600, or on the Web at *www.copyright.com*. Requests to the Publisher for permission should be addressed to the Permissions Department, John Wiley & Sons, Inc., 111 River Street, Hoboken, NJ 07030, 201-748-6011, fax 201-748-6008.

Limit of Liability/Disclaimer of Warranty: While the publisher and author have used their best efforts in preparing this book, they make no representations or warranties with respect to the accuracy or completeness of the contents of this book and specifically disclaim any implied warranties of merchantability or fitness for a particular purpose. No warranty may be created or extended by sales representatives or written sales materials. The advice and strategies contained herein may not be suitable for your situation. You should consult with a professional where appropriate. Neither the publisher nor author shall be liable for any loss of profit or any other commercial damages, including but not limited to special, incidental, consequential, or other damages.

For general information on our other products and services, or technical support, please contact our Customer Care Department within the United States at 800-762-2974, outside the United States at 317-572-3993 or fax 317-572-4002.

Wiley also publishes its books in a variety of electronic formats. Some content that appears in print may not be available in electronic books.

For more information about Wiley products, visit our Web site at *www.wiley.com*.

Library of Congress Cataloging-in-Publication Data:

Schaeffer, Mary S.
    Accounts payable best practices / Mary S. Schaeffer.
        p. cm.
"Published simultaneously in Canada."
Includes index.
    ISBN 0-471-63695-9 (cloth : alk. paper)
    1. Accounts payable. I. Title.
HF5681.A27 S3 2004
658.15′26—dc22

                                                              2003026689

10 9 8 7 6 5 4 3 2 1

For my candle in the wind,
my father,
Ron Schacht

Contents

Contents

Contents

Contents

Introduction

Companies should be interested in implementing best practices in their accounts payable (AP) operations for the same reason that Willy Sutton focused on banks—it's where the money is. The fundamental structure of the AP function is that it is about a company's financial integrity. Those who disregard their AP operations will adversely affect their bottom line, either directly by

- Paying invoices more than once
- Paying charges that should have been borne by the supplier
- Failing to take advantage of special pricing arrangements
- Not taking earned discounts
- Being fined by states for failing to comply with escheat or sales and tax rules

or indirectly through

- Increased transactional costs
- Increased costs to resolve discrepancies
- Increased costs to fix errors
- Increased costs by failing to take advantage of new processes and technologies
- Failing to earn early payment discounts

OVERVIEW: FACTORS

The AP function has changed radically over the last 10 years, and it appears that the transformation will continue at least for the foreseeable future. The following are some of the factors affecting this transformation:

- Check fraud had reached levels that demanded not only a change in the way companies write checks but also the technology used to limit the scams.
- Companies looking for ways to keep costs under control have cut AP staffs to the bone.
- Technology has made a big dent in the amount of resources companies now need to allocate to transactional work.
- The concentration in a growing number of accounts payable operations is shifting from transactional processing to an analytical focus.
- The overall number of people working in AP is declining. That decrease is almost entirely in the clerical staff. Consequently, the professional level of these departments is rising.
- States, desperate for ways to increase their coffers without alienating the voters, have found companies failing to comply with unclaimed property and sales and use tax rules to be just the answer to their problems. They are aggressively pursuing them and, when they find them in noncompliance, auditing and fining them uncompromisingly. States now use third-party auditors in many cases. They also work together.
- The accounting scandals and the enactment of the Sarbanes-Oxley Act have raised the level of inspection at many companies, both private and public.
- The Internet

BEST PRACTICE PRINCIPLES

With reduced resources and increased scrutiny, implementing best practices in AP is more crucial than ever. Strictly focusing on cost is apt to get a company into trouble. While keeping costs down is a good idea, it is important not to let that be the only consideration. It is important that sufficient thought also be given to adequate controls, fraud prevention, and good vendor relationships.

To that end, in defining best practices, the following over-riding principles will govern:

- Up-front controls
- A move toward minimizing paper
- Clear and easily traceable audit trails
- Minimal clerical data entry
- Transactional efficiency

This should translate into lower costs, in most instances.

BEST PRACTICES IN A THEORETICAL BEST PRACTICE COMPANY

If it were possible to select best practices simply on the basis of what's best and not taking into account corporate culture, existing procedures, financial limitations, and unique corporate procedures, here's what the list might look like:

- Implement e-invoicing for all invoicing.
- Use positive pay.
- Insist that all purchase orders be completely filled out before they are issued, and that Receiving completely check packing slips.
- Use workflow to route invoices for reviews with an escalating approval structure.

- Have travel and entertainment (T&E) reports completed electronically; spot check rather than completely review each report; and make all employee reimbursements using direct deposit.
- Comply with all escheat and sales and use tax regulations.
- Make every payment possible electronically.
- Encourage all employees to be paid via direct deposit.
- Take advantage of all early payment discounts, but don't make any payments before the due date.
- Provide adequate resources for employee continuing education opportunities.

IMPLEMENTING BEST ACCOUNTS PAYABLE PRACTICE POLICIES

While the rest of this book examines AP functions in detail and spells out the best practices for each, this section will look at some overall best practice policies:

- Minimize or eliminate low-dollar invoices. This can be done through a variety of techniques, including:
  - Use of purchase cards (p-cards)
  - Making payments to certain vendors from statements rather than invoices
  - E-invoicing
- Institute strong up-front controls, eliminating the most back-end approval processes:
  - Completely filled-out purchase orders
  - Evaluated receipt settlement
  - Negative assurance
- Get rid of as much paper as possible using:
  - Imaging

- E-invoicing
- A firm policy regarding where invoices should be sent first
- P-cards
- Consider outsourcing specialty functions, including:
  - Sales and use tax
  - Escheat
  - Duplicate payment audits
  - Value-added tax reclaim
  - Telecom and freight payment and audits
- Make as many payments as possible electronically, using:
  - Direct deposit
  - Automated clearinghouse credits and, where appropriate, debits
- Limit the number of phone calls coming into AP by:
  - Using online dispute resolution
  - Updating payment status on the Internet
  - Updating payment status using interactive voice response (IVR)
  - Publicizing payment timetables
  - Including an explanation slip with all short payments
- Don't forget the value employees bring to the AP function:
  - Motivate staff
  - Focus on morale
  - Allocate some resources for staff education

A WORD ABOUT BEST PRACTICES

It's fine to talk about best practices in a theoretical sense, but professionals who toil in the field know that sometimes what works in theory will not work in their organization. Sometimes industry peculiarities stand in the way, and other times it might be the corporate culture or practices in another department. If the receiving dock does not do a good job at checking packing slips, it is pointless to implement a process that relies on accurate information from Receiving.

Thus, in this book, you will see discussions of best practices as well as what we refer to as "almost best practices." These take into account that not all practices will work at all companies and offer an alternative to those who cannot implement the absolutely best practices.

We also include a discussion of those practices that definitely should not be used but, as many reading this know from painful experience, are in use in parts of Corporate America. Hopefully, by seeing these practices identified in print, some will decide to replace them in their own organizations.

WHAT'S INSIDE

The book starts at the beginning, reviewing the way invoices are processed. It identifies a number of potential problem areas and then offers best practice solutions. Some of the items may seem mundane to those not intimately familiar with AP. However, if they are ignored, expect duplicate payments and perhaps even fraud to increase.

At least for the present, as most AP departments have not made the leap to 100 percent electronic payments, checks dominate the payment landscape. If all aspects of this function are not handled properly, check fraud, duplicate payments, and processing costs will all increase. Also, the company may put itself in the position of being completely liable for any check fraud that does occur.

The mundane operational aspects of AP are reviewed in a way that focuses attention on issues that are sometimes ignored. A complete chapter follows this on one of the most important, yet overlooked aspects of the purchase-to-pay cycle—the master vendor file. You would be surprised how often the master vendor file is not even an issue on the table—with disastrous consequences. With the renewed interest in internal audit and controls, thanks to the Sarbanes-Oxley Act, companies disregard their master vendor file at their own peril.

P-cards are one of the easiest innovations to understand, and companies everywhere are adopting them. The potential for growth in this area is staggering. Thus, it is imperative that those who use them do so correctly. The cost and time savings will be maximized if best practices are implemented from the beginning.

T&E is an area that has changed dramatically in the last decade. Online filing, the increased use of T&E cards, and other electronic initiatives have changed the way most of corporate America handles their T&E function. The chapter on T&E reveals some of the techniques used at innovative companies.

While few people think of AP and regulatory issues in the same breath, there are a few issues that, if not handled correctly, can bring trouble to a company. Specifically, in this chapter we take a look at 1099 reporting, sales and use tax handling and reporting, and unclaimed property, also called escheat. It is the last two areas, sometimes ignored by companies, that are drawing increased attention from the states.

As the AP function becomes more analytical, it is inevitable that companies begin to expect that the professionals who run AP take a cash management approach to the function. In some ways, paying too early is just as bad as paying too late. This chapter takes a look at some of the cash management initiatives that are increasingly falling on the shoulders of the AP department.

Although in many cases, AP was one of the last groups within some companies to get computers, they are making up for it in a big way today. Technology is making inroads into the department in an extraordinary manner. This chapter shares some of those innovations. We expect this area to continue to expand, especially as AP takes the lead in pushing for electronic invoicing and a move to electronic payments—away from the check standard.

Finally, successful AP departments are starting to realize that they have customers—both internal and external. By finding ways to deal with both, they are also improving vendor relationships. Those that do not make this leap can hurt the vendor relationship and increase costs as poor communications with other departments run up the dispute resolution bill.

Upon looking back at the items covered, it is truly amazing how much AP has changed in the last 5 to 10 years. This book attempts to identify the best practices that will make your AP department first rate.

1

Invoices

Invoices can present a real challenge to the payment function. If any of the aspects are not handled correctly, the payment process bogs down. In this chapter, we'll look at

- Invoice handling: approvals
- Forwarding invoices
- Verifying invoice data
- Invoice-coding standards
- Short-paying invoices
- Paying small-dollar invoices
- Handling unidentified invoices
- Handling invoices without invoice numbers

INVOICE HANDLING: APPROVALS

Background

As most reading this are well aware, Accounts Payable (AP) does a three-way match before paying an invoice. This entails matching the

- Purchase order (PO)
- Invoice
- Packing slip

In theory, if all POs are filled out completely and correctly, if receiving thoroughly checks all packing slips, and vendors create accurate invoices, the AP department should be able to pay the invoice without input from any other party. However, few companies are at this point. Even at those companies in which the documentation is good, management often demands that the original purchaser get involved and approve the invoice for payment. Part of the reasoning for this is that often POs are not completely filled out and special pricing or payment deals are not reflected on the PO. Unfortunately, the purchaser who neglects to include special terms on the PO is just as likely to forget about them when the invoice shows up.

With no formal policy governing where invoices are sent, first invoices sometimes float around the corporation, laying the groundwork for all sorts of poor practices. For starters, the invoice often fails to arrive in any location that could process it before the end of the early discount period. Additionally, it provides cover for those approvers who tend to let the invoice lie on their desk for weeks without taking action. Then, when the supplier is threatening to put the company on credit hold, these individuals deceitfully claim that they "sent that invoice down to Accounts Payable for processing weeks ago."

Recent innovations in the area of electronic invoicing are rapidly changing the way we think about invoices. This is reflected in some of the following recommendations.

Best Practices

At most companies, only certain people can approve invoices for payment. Most companies limit this ability by rank, job re-

2

sponsibility, type of purchase, and sometimes even the dollar amount. In the best of circumstances, the board of directors should have given these approvers authority, and AP should have copies of these board authorizations.

Copies of the list, if it exists in paper format, should be given only to those who need it, and in all cases should be filed away carefully. The list should not be hung on the wall for easy reference or left lying on a desk where anyone walking by could see it and easily make a copy. When the list is updated, as it periodically will be, old copies of the list should be destroyed.

If you want to be super careful, new copies of the list should only be exchanged for the old ones, and all the old ones can be destroyed together.

The fact that an invoice arrives in Accounts Payable with a senior executive's signature on it does not mean that the senior executive actually approved the invoice. To protect the AP staff, the department should have signature cards containing the actual signature of anyone authorized to approve invoices. It should be the executive's real signature, the one he or she uses every day, and not the Sunday-school signature. More than one executive has taken the time to sign a signature card carefully, when in actuality everything else has an illegible scrawl on it. In these cases, the signature card should have the illegible scrawl as well, or the AP associate might suspect fraud when the signature cards are checked.

We are not suggesting that these cards be checked for every invoice that shows up. However, spot checking once in a while is not a bad idea. And, obviously, if a suspicious-looking signature arrives on an invoice, the signature cards should be checked immediately.

Ideally, invoices will arrive electronically. Admittedly, today, only a small portion of invoices is received electronically, but that number is growing by leaps and bounds. When an invoice is received electronically, it should be forwarded to AP for processing. Using workflow, the AP department can forward the invoice for approval to the appropriate approver. This is based on information provided on the invoice integrated with the approver list discussed earlier.

Companies should include in their workflow programming an escalating approval feature. What this means is that if the first approver does not respond within a given time frame, say five days, the invoice is automatically routed to the next higher approver in that chain of command. This not only takes care of tardy approvers, but also vacations and unexpected absences. It simultaneously creates an audit trail for everyone to see. No longer can Purchasing claim it sent an invoice back to AP when it is still in the department. Finally, the audit trail feature combined with escalating approvals make it far less likely that managers will relegate invoice approval to the bottom of their workload—especially when not approving invoices may actually create more work for their immediate supervisors.

When companies receive paper invoices, as virtually every company does, the invoices should be directed to AP rather than the individual purchasers. This allows AP to log the invoice in and forward it to the appropriate approver. It helps get a handle on the voluminous paper that can spread throughout a company without any boundaries. Ideally, when all invoices are directed to AP, they can then be scanned and forwarded, as described above, for approvals. Even if the intricate workflow programming is not feasible, there is still some audit trail and the number of lost invoices is greatly reduced. The invoice never leaves AP, and thus the "opportunity" to get lost on someone's desk or in the mail is diminished. In order to make such a process work efficiently, vendors should be directed to include the name of the purchaser on all invoices. Companies that make this process work the best are those that send invoices without the purchaser's name back to the vendor.

Having all invoices come first to AP also introduces another control against employee fraud. Invoices cannot be altered, nor can they show up out of the blue with what looks like an executive's signature on them. By scanning the invoices and forwarding them for approval, it makes it all the harder for a scheming employee to forge a boss's signature.

Almost Best Practices

In the absence of board authorizations, AP should have a list of who can approve what purchases. A high-level executive at the company should sign off on this list. Otherwise, it is exceedingly easy to have fraud, and AP could end up taking on a responsibility it should not.

If it is not possible to get imaging—even an inexpensive model—in AP, a policy still should be set up for receiving invoices. If all the invoices come to AP first, it will be necessary to set up a log to track which invoices were received, their due dates, and whom they were sent to for approvals. This can be a tedious and time-consuming, paper-intensive process—as copies should be made of the invoices before they are sent out for approval.

Having the invoices come first to AP helps with the possible employee fraud issue discussed earlier.

Reality Check for Accounts Payable

While sending invoices lacking the purchaser's name back to suppliers may lead to a smoother AP operation, not all management teams are going to think this is a great idea—especially if key suppliers balk or complain. Thus, it might be a good idea to get management on board before instituting this policy.

Worst Practices

Worst practices include

- Having no policy regarding where invoices should be sent for payment

- Not having a list of authorized approvers
- Allowing anyone to submit invoices for payment.

FORWARDING INVOICES

Background

On the face of it, it would seem that where invoices were mailed should have little impact on the payment function. Unfortunately, this is not the case. In a typical company with no invoice forwarding policy, invoices that are addressed to the company but not a particular individual can float for weeks from desk to desk before eventually ending up in AP or on the desk of the purchaser. When invoices are not properly routed,

- Any chance of earning an early payment discount is lost.
- Duplicate payments can occur when a second invoice is sent.
- Late fees can occur.
- Vendor relations are weakened.

Best Practices

Companies need to have a firm policy regarding where invoices should be sent. This can be one of two places:

1. The AP department
2. The original purchaser

Either way works just as long as there is consistency in the approach. There is a slight advantage of directing all invoices to AP. When the invoices are sent directly to AP, a best practice is to insist that the purchaser's name be included on the invoice so the AP staff knows where to forward the invoice for approval. Some companies adhere to this approach, strictly returning invoices to vendors if they arrive without the requestor's name.

The appeal of sending the invoice to AP first is that AP can easily track invoices. The downside is that, if electronic invoicing is not used, AP needs to make copies of the invoices before forwarding them for approval unless the following are used:

- Scanning
- Negative assurance
- Assumed receipt

If the invoice is sent first to the original purchaser, AP may find itself inundated with "Where's my money?" and "Did you get my invoice yet?" calls. However, many simply advise the caller to telephone the purchaser.

Electronic invoicing (e-invoicing) eliminates this problem completely.

Almost Best Practices

Direct the mailroom to forward all invoices—regardless of whom they are addressed to—to the AP department for processing.

Reality Check for Accounts Payable

Even with the advent of e-invoicing, paper invoices will be here for the foreseeable future, although hopefully in smaller numbers. Thus, it is imperative that a policy for forwarding invoices be established.

Worst Practices

Worst practices include having no policy on this issue.

VERIFYING INVOICE DATA

Background

In an ideal world a company would sell its customers products and would in due course be paid for those goods according to the prenegotiated payment terms, once the purchaser had verified that it had received what it had ordered. (Some reading this may recognize this as the underlying principle of evaluated receipt settlement [ERS].) Unfortunately, there is a lot that can and often does go wrong with this simple scenario. Some of the things that go awry include

- Terms on the invoice not matching what was negotiated
- Partial shipments
- Damaged goods
- Prices on the invoice not matching the negotiated prices
- Inclusion or exclusion of related charges such as freight, insurance, and so on
- Sales and use tax charged/not charged

Consequently, the process for paying for goods can be complicated, especially when it comes to verifying the suppliers' invoices.

Best Practices

Once the invoice has been approved (if that is required), a three-way match should be performed on all invoices over some minimal level. Small-dollar invoices will be addressed further on. The AP associate should match the PO against the invoice and packing slip to verify that the goods ordered have been received and the price and other fees (e.g., tax, insurance, freight) are as agreed.

Differences must be resolved before the invoice can be

paid. If the difference is in the pricing, the better price should be taken. If the lower price happens to be on the PO, not only should the lower price be taken, but Purchasing should be notified as well. The reasoning for this is that if a lower price is put on an invoice, it probably indicates that the supplier is offering a lower price to other customers and Purchasing should pursue that for your company.

Accounts Payable can do a good job on this issue—especially when it comes to terms, insurance, freight, and so on—only if the PO is completely filled out. Often, Purchasing does not include special deals on the PO, and AP never knows about it. If the supplier does not include the special terms on the invoice—and this often happens—AP will pay according to the standard terms or pricing, and the company is the loser. Thus, a best practice that needs to be emphasized with Purchasing is that POs must be completely filled out.

The process described above can be done online. The best systems now have online dispute resolution features built in, especially when using e-invoicing.

As mentioned earlier, some companies use a process known as evaluated receipt settlement (ERS). This eliminates the invoice from the process—the document that many AP professionals believe causes the most problems with the three-way match. Using ERS, the AP staff receives POs from Purchasing, and when it gets the packing slip from receiving, it pays according to the terms indicated on the PO. Companies that insist that the PO be completely and accurately filled out have taken the first step toward being able to get rid of the invoice. If the PO line is under control and the professionals on the receiving dock thoroughly check the packing slips on incoming orders, a company could effectively use ERS. Use of ERS has to be negotiated with suppliers before implementing. This is also known as pay-on-receipt.

In addition to verifying that the PO matches the invoice regarding price and other fees, many companies are now taking the verification process one step further with a contract management function. As the title implies, invoices, sometimes after the fact, are checked against contracts to ensure that pricing, terms, and so on are charged as agreed upon in the master contract agreement. This typically occurs only with major suppliers.

Almost Best Practices

Obviously, going through a thorough three-way match can be an expensive process for small-dollar invoices. There is an alternative. First, the company must set a dollar cutoff for use of one of the alternatives. This cutoff can be as low as $100 or as high as $5,000 or $25,000. Companies that institute one of the following can start small and then increase the level as they get comfortable with the process. Corporate culture will also have an impact.

The first approach is referred to as negative assurance or assumed receipt. When AP gets an invoice for an amount under the agreed-on level, an e-mail is sent to the person who would approve the invoice, indicating key factors, such as payee, dollar amount, and so on. If imaging is being used, a copy of the invoice can be attached to the e-mail message. If AP does not hear from the approver within a preset number of days—typically 5 to 10 days—the invoice is paid. The goods are assumed to have been received unless the purchaser notifies AP to the contrary.

Reality Check for Accounts Payable

Many approvers don't check the information on invoices, nor do they bother to verify that the invoice they are approving today wasn't approved last week or last month. That's part of the reason so many duplicate payments occur.

Worst Practices

Worst practices include

- Allowing Purchasing to send POs to Accounts Payable without complete and accurate information
- Not following some of the best practices described under the "Duplicate Payment Avoidance" section in Chapter 3.

INVOICE-CODING STANDARDS

Background

Coding invoices is one of those functions that no one really focuses on too much. However, handled ineffectually, it can and does lead to duplicate payments and opens the door to fraud. It is one of those functions that at first glance seem like a non-issue. What do you mean you want standards for coding invoices? The words *control freak* may be running through your mind. But consider the following simple case. Consider the company AT&T. Its name could be coded:

- American Telephone and Telegraph
- AT&T
- A T & T
- A T and T

Even if you eliminate the first entry as unlikely, it is easy to see how two competent AP specialists could code the company name in any one of several ways, none of which would be inaccurate. Each data element has similar issues.

Best Practices

Taking the process one step further, consider the invoice number. As those familiar with AP are well aware, the invoice number is crucial for identifying potential duplicate payments. Thus, it must be coded correctly. Do you code leading zeros or not? There is no right or wrong answer. Each company must decide if it wants to code them and then set a policy. Each aspect of invoice-coding policy should be addressed, a policy set, and then communicated to all processors. It may seem excessive, but it will eliminate numerous problems down the road.

Presented below is a policy developed by Apex Analytic's Jim Arnold. It is a good policy but definitely not the only one that works. Readers can use it or modify it to meet their own requirements.

Sample Policy: Dos and Don'ts for Invoice Coding

- No periods (.), commas (,), or other punctuation marks (e.g., ! or /) keyed into the invoice number field

VALID	INVALID
S19408C004	S/19408C004

- No leading zeros keyed into the invoice number field

VALID	INVALID
S19408C004	000S19408C004

- No spaces keyed before, in between, or after the invoice number

VALID	INVALID
S19408C004	S 19408C004

- No symbols or characters including dashes (-) and apostrophes ('), keyed into the invoice number field

VALID	INVALID
S19408C004	S-19408C004

- Alphanumeric invoices should *not* be modified if alpha characters are a true part of the invoice number. Beware of field names or labels, such as INV, IN, or NO that are seen before or after the true invoice number and do not include them as a part of the invoice number.

  VALID   **INVALID**
  S19408C004   INV S19408C004

- If the invoice number exceeds the maximum number of digits in the invoice number field, utilize the maximum number of digits starting from the far right and going left (by starting to the right you are ensuring that the unique sequential numbering scheme is utilized as the invoice number).

  ACTUAL INV #   **VALID**   **INVALID**
  P1001S19408C004   S19408C004   P1001S1940

- Establish a standard invoice numbering scheme for re-curring payments such as utilities, or monthly state-ments that don't have a true invoice number. If the ac-count or customer number is provided, begin the invoice number with the account number + the month + year as a suffix at the end in MMYY format. For weekly statement billings, also include the day so the invoice number will equal the account, or customer number + month + day + year suffix in the MMDDYY format. For telephone services, use the telephone number starting with the area code + phone number + month + year suf-fix in MMYY format.

  VALID   **INVALID**
  33627246691202   336272466902

- For invoices with a true invoice number, do not add alpha or numeric characters to the invoice number. (See following exceptions.)

VALID	**INVALID**
S19408C004	RRS19408C004

- Sometimes invoice numbers must be altered to identify separate items or balances due. Establish a policy that outlines these exceptions. Examples include
  - *Sales tax paid separately.* Alter invoice number by adding the suffix "TX".
  - *GST paid separately.* Alter invoice number by adding the suffix "GST".
  - *Credit on invoice.* Alter invoice number by adding the suffix "CR".
  - *Freight paid separately.* Alter invoice number by adding the suffix "FRT".
  - *Balance due.* Alter invoice number by adding the suffix "BD".
  - *Split invoice for payment.* Alter invoice number by adding the suffix "A", "B", and so on.
  - *Prepayment.* Alter invoice number by adding the suffix "PP".

- Establish a standard procedure that outlines the alternative information to be used as invoice numbers when a true invoice number does not exist. For example:
  - *Subscriptions.* For subscriptions that do not have an invoice number, use the subscriber's last name + first name initial + date of the statement in MMDDYY format.

VALID	SmithJ010102

14

- *Hotel invoices.* For hotel bills that don't have an invoice number, use the folio number + the last day of the stay in MMDDYY format.
  VALID   55246010102

- *Tuition, seminars, or conferences.* For these items that don't have an invoice number, use the attendee's last name + first name initial + the last day of the event in date format MMDDYY. For tuition, utilize the student's last name + first name initial + semester + year in YY format.
  VALID   SmithJFall02

- If the invoice has other tracking information and no invoice number, use one of the alternatives. Alternative invoice numbers may include order number, document number, reference number, registration number, billing number, item number, job number, membership number, and so on. In case more than one of these identifiers exists, have a policy that identifies which information should be used. Preference in order, for example, could be (1) order number, (2) billing number, and so forth.

- Review your AP and purchasing systems to identify unique internal identifiers for processing petty cash, postmaster, or budgeted amounts such as grants and contributions that would assist in the invoice numbering sequence to eliminate duplicate payments and give each item processed in AP a distinctive identity.

- Only as a last resort use the date that exists on the attached vendor documentation as the invoice number. Do not use the due date. Avoid using the check request date whenever possible. Date format should be MMDDYY.

- Handwritten changes to the true invoice number should not be utilized.

Note: The invoice-coding standard should be coordinated with the master vendor file coding/naming policy. Ideally, the two should handle the same issue in the same manner.

Almost Best Practices

- If no invoice-coding standard exists, use the standard naming convention used when setting up master vendor files. Although it is not perfect—it doesn't address certain issues peculiar to invoices—it is better than nothing.
- If an invoice-coding standard does not exist, at a minimum, establish policies for coding the invoice number. If various staffers code invoice numbers differently, duplicates will seep into the process.

Reality Check for Accounts Payable

Even with a clear policy, processors will occasionally veer off. As soon as this is noticed, the AP manager needs to correct the situation; without conformity on this issue, duplicate payments will slip through. If the thought process behind the policy is explained, most processors will understand and abide by it.

Worst Practices

Worst practices include not having a policy at all. Each processor will use his or her best judgment, leading to duplicate payments.

SHORT-PAYING INVOICES

Background

When most companies print their checks, they print identifying information on the accompanying remittance advice. The most important piece of information usually is the invoice number. It gives the vendor the information it needs to apply the cash to the correct account. Certain companies send along a stub with their bills. They require that this stub be returned with the payment. This is so the vendor can apply the cash payment correctly.

However, as those reading this are well aware, the amount of information that can be included on a remittance advice is severely limited. When an invoice is short paid, and the reasons for that are not communicated to the vendor, it is inevitable that the vendor will call AP for an explanation. Unfortunately, by the time the vendor gets around to calling, days, if not weeks, will have passed and the AP associate will have long forgotten why the deduction was taken—assuming that the person getting the call was the person responsible for the deduction in the first place.

Deductions are frequently made for various reasons, including

- Discounts for early payment
- Short shipments
- Damaged goods
- Advertising allowances
- Prior credits
- Insurance or freight incorrectly charged
- Pricing adjustments
- Overshipments
- Advertising allowances

Best Practices

Whenever invoices are not paid in full, it is important—not only to keep the AP department running smoothly, but also to help maintain good vendor relationships—that the reasons for the deductions be communicated in as much detail as possible to the vendor. This does not ensure that the vendor will agree or won't call, but it will eliminate many needless calls. Thus, even though it might take a little extra time when the invoices are being processed, put detailed notes in the file as to the reason for the deductions. This can be important if the matter is raised after several months or in the case of an audit. The detailed notes will be worth their weight in gold.

The best approach is to include a detailed breakdown for the reasons for the deductions. Those making electronic payments will find that this information can often be shared as part of the electronic remittance advice. Alternatively, it can be e-mailed to the person at the vendor doing the cash applications.

Almost Best Practices

A low-tech approach, especially useful with payments made by check is to develop a form that lists the most common reasons for short payments. Then the AP associate can simply check off the appropriate field and attach it to the check. These forms should be developed based on the company's past history and industry. They should be periodically reviewed to ensure that they contain all relevant factors. There should be several blank lines at the bottom for any details that will be useful to those using the form.

There is a small group of accounts payable organizations that never short pay an invoice. They hold the view that they will not pay an invoice until it is prepared correctly. They return these invoices demanding that the supplier correct them and when the invoice is prepared to their satisfaction, they pay it. While this approach does hold great appeal, it is not one that will work in most organizations.

Reality Check for Accounts Payable

Don't expect that the form will put an end to vendors' complaints. It will simply eliminate one round of calls and one round of investigations as the information typically provided in that round will have been provided on the form.

Worst Practices

Worst practices include sending along a short payment with no explanation. The vendor will call and, even worse, may end up putting the company on credit hold thinking it is owed money—funds that were legitimately deducted from a payment. The name of the game in this case is communication—you can't have too much of it.

PAYING SMALL-DOLLAR INVOICES

Background

Small-dollar invoices are the bane of every AP department. With estimates ranging as high as $50 to process an invoice, it does not make a whole lot of sense to process hundreds of small-dollar invoices each day. Yet, that is precisely what happens in numerous accounts payable organizations across the country every day.

Getting an invoice for a $10 purchase makes little sense to either the seller who has to produce the invoice, mail it to the customer, track its payment status, apply the cash, and then maintain a bank account to process the payment. Similarly, processing an invoice, getting approvals, cutting a check, getting that check signed and mailed makes even less sense for the purchaser.

While both sides may agree that the transaction described above doesn't make a whole lot of sense, many still engage in it every day. There are better ways.

Best Practices

The goal is to find ways to eliminate invoices for small-dollar purchases. To put this issue in perspective, begin by doing an analysis of the enterprise expenditure by invoice amount. If your company is anything like most firms, you will discover that the old 80–20 rule kicks in. With 80 percent of the invoice volume covering 20 percent (or less) of the total spend, companies that don't take advantage of some of the newer alternative strategies are not making the most of their AP resources. All of the following strategies will help eliminate small-dollar invoices:

- Use purchase cards (p-cards) to eliminate all small-dollar invoices.
- Move small-dollar invoices to e-invoicing approaches, especially for those vendors who submit numerous invoices.
- Move to summary billing. Paying from statements (for those suppliers who have many small-dollar invoices). Once payments are to be made from statements, no invoices from the statement suppliers should be honored.
- Have the supplier send along an Excel spreadsheet (once a day, week, or month, as appropriate) and upload the information for processing.
- Have employees who submit small-dollar invoices, pay them themselves and include the items on their travel and entertainment (T&E) reports for reimbursement purposes.

While not all the strategies suggested will work at all companies, several should help most get their small-dollar invoice problems under control.

Some companies, and again this is something that not all companies are willing to do, take an aggressive approach to small-dollar invoices. When an invoice is submitted for payment that could have been paid using one of the strategies discussed above, that invoice is returned to the submitter with instructions on how to pay the invoice. While this does take additional time and effort on the part of the AP associate processing the invoice, in the long term it trains employees on the correct way to handle small-dollar invoices.

Almost Best Practices

Should the company have a petty cash box (heaven forbid), small-dollar invoices can be funded from the box with an employee paying the invoice with his own credit card.

Reality Check for Accounts Payable

No matter how hard the AP staff works to completely eliminate small-dollar invoices, they will appear—and have to be processed. The goal is to minimize these annoyances.

Worst Practices

Worst practices include taking no action with these annoying invoices.

HANDLING UNIDENTIFIED INVOICES

Background

Frequently, an invoice will show up in the AP department with no identification as to who ordered the product. Occasionally, these invoices will float from desk to desk throughout the company before finding their way into AP. Sometimes, by looking at what is included on the invoice, a savvy AP associate will be able to figure out who the likely purchaser is and will then forward the invoice to that person for approval.

However, that is frequently not the case, especially in the case of generic goods like printer cartridges or paper for the copy machine. Often, the dollar amount involved is small and does not appear to be worth the time and effort to research who ordered the goods.

Best Practices

The best approach, although one that not every management team is comfortable with, is to send these unidentified invoices back to the sender, asking them to indicate who ordered the goods. This is especially important in the case of small-dollar items. (See the "Worst Practices" section.)

Almost Best Practices

If it is not feasible to simply return the invoice, pick up the phone and call the vendor. When provided with the information, request that in the future the vendor include the requestors' names on invoices. If this is a recurring problem, keep a list of vendors who routinely omit the purchasers' name along with the employees' names who regularly order from these companies. Again, ask the employees to request that their name or department be included on all invoices.

Reality Check for Accounts Payable

This is one of those headaches that in all likelihood will never go away completely. However, AP should do what it can to minimize the problem. By working with these suppliers, many of whom are small and will be amenable to listening to suggestions (rather than demands) and employees, AP will be able to make a dent in the problem.

Worst Practices

Worst practices include simply paying for the goods, reasoning that the dollar amount is too small to bother with. This can quickly get your company on the sucker list. More than a few companies out there prey on overworked AP departments. They send along invoices for goods not ordered, knowing full well that small-dollar invoices are often paid without authorization. Once you pay that unidentified invoice, your company will be hit over and over again—and probably for increasingly larger amounts of money as time goes on.

HANDLING INVOICES WITHOUT INVOICE NUMBERS

Background

Invoice numbers are extremely important when it comes to processing invoices. They are the primary way that most companies identify invoices and check to see if they have already paid a particular item. An invoice without an invoice number is much more likely to be paid twice than one that has this key identifier. Yet a large number of invoices routinely arrive without invoice numbers, creating all sorts of headaches for the companies that receive them.

That's just the beginning of the problems. When the customer goes through its computer files, it will search to see if the particular invoice number has been paid. Additionally, most accounting programs require an invoice number in order to generate a payment.

So, to get around these problems, most companies assign invoice numbers to those invoices that arrive without these important identifiers. If not done in a manner that will create unique identifiers, the system will regularly dump out a large number of payments when any duplicate payment check programs are run. The key is to do it in a manner that does not create more problems that it solves.

Best Practices

The important facet of this discussion is to recognize that invoices without invoice numbers are a problem and to devise a system to deal with the issue that does not create additional problems at the same time. The best technique is probably to make up a dummy number that includes some unique identifier to the vendor, for example, a combination of digits from the vendor's phone number and a running total.

If you are a large customer of a smaller vendor, you may be in a position to impose your will and get that vendor to incorporate some best practices in its operations. Recommend (insist?) that it start putting unique invoice numbers on its invoices.

Almost Best Practices

Another ploy is to use a combination of the account number from the master vendor file and the date. This works well for those vendors who do not send in more than one invoice per day. However, it will fail at those companies that have the potential to receive more than one invoice per day from a vendor, for example, temporary employment firms and so on.

Reality Check for Accounts Payable

Invoices without invoice numbers create huge headaches in AP. Even if you have a wonderful system for creating an invoice number, that number will not be of any use when discussing open items with the vendor as it does not know the invoice number and if you refer to that identifier, the vendor will have no idea what you are talking about.

Worst Practices

Using the date to assign an invoice number is likely to cause problems, as you will probably end up with duplicate invoice numbers. Some use a combination of the vendor number and the date. Again, this can cause trouble if you receive more than one invoice from the same vendor on the same day.

Creating an invoice number using the account number when it bears any relation to the taxpayer identification number or a person's Social Security number also can cause problems. There have been instances in which unscrupulous employees (yes, there are a few of those) have taken the Social Security numbers and used them in an unethical manner.

CASE STUDY

How One Pro Took Accounts Payable Out of the Picture when Resolving Customer Discrepancies

Does your AP staff waste endless hours trying to resolve discrepancies with the Purchasing department? Jim Heard at Dana Corporation found a great way to solve this problem. The company refers to the mechanism as a trouble board. "The trouble board," says Heard, "is a communication tool between accounts payable specialists and buyers. Since there can be more than one buyer at a plant, there are multiple trouble boards, one for each buyer code on our system." What happens if one buyer uses more than one code? Heard says the company has the ability to combine these into one trouble board to simplify its maintenance of the system.

PURPOSE OF THE BOARDS

If the three-way match were perfect, there would be no need for Heard's trouble boards. However, as those reading this are well aware, there are often discrepancies in the three-way match. The rationale behind the trouble board was to give each buyer hands-on ability to approve an option of payment necessitated as a result of a mismatch of the three-way match. In other words, explains Heard, quantities or prices on the PO are different from those on the invoice. The boards deleted faxes and phone calls to the buyers across the United States and eliminated duplication of handling in cases in which the buyer approves invoice quantities and prices.

There are additional benefits to the AP department. The trouble board items do not require additional handling by an AP specialist. "Once the buyer approves the invoice," says Heard, "it is transmitted to Dana Corporate for payment the day after the buyer gives the approval." This entails no additional effort on the part of the AP department.

APPROVAL DIFFERENT FROM THE INVOICE

As those who work in AP know, paying an amount different from the dollar amount indicated on the invoice can create huge headaches at a later date. But not at Dana Corporation. "In the case where a buyer approves receiver quantities or PO pricing contrary to invoicing, the system creates a debit memo or credit memo to properly carry out the buyer's decision, but the item is put on hold pending accounts payable specialist handling," explains Heard. He says that the reason for this approach is the possibility of additional charges needing to be added to the automatic memo to recover freight or taxes that could not be automatically calculated within the system.

WHAT'S NEEDED TO IMPLEMENT A TROUBLE BOARD

While this sounds like a great idea, not every company will be able to implement the model exactly the way Dana Corporation did. "The whole concept of a trouble board," says Heard, "was made possible by the availability of electronic POs and receipts within the system." He says that Purchasing employees resisted the change, but after two years, it is well accepted.

There is another reason the trouble boards work well. A tolerance exists within the system that allows the company to place parameters within the system to keep petty discrepancies from hitting the trouble board.

FUTURE ENHANCEMENTS

Heard is always looking for ways to make existing processes work better. Another reason for allowing the tolerances was that the boards are plant specific, not supplier specific. The variation and mix of merchandise being purchased is best served by a supplier-specific tolerance.

Heard plans to address this issue in the near term, which he defines as within the next three to four years, depending on information technology (IT) resources. Why so long? "Once a system functions, enhancements such as this take a back seat to implementations in progress. Over the next year, implementations and enhancements will be hard to come by," he explains.

2

Checks

Although pundits have long predicted the demise of the paper check, they are still with us, causing Accounts Payable a myriad of headaches. Although the number of checks issued each year has finally begun to decline, they will be with AP for the foreseeable future. In this chapter, we investigate best check practices in the following areas:

- Check printing
- Check signing
- Check storage
- Distribution of checks
- Check fraud/positive pay
- Rush/ASAP or emergency checks

CHECK PRINTING

Background

Companies print checks as frequently as every day and as infrequently as once or twice a month, depending on numerous factors, which can include

- Corporate culture
- Cash management practices
- Number of checks printed
- Check-signing practices
- Check-printing practices
- Efficiencies in the invoice handling procedures

As bizarre as it may seem, a few companies print checks only once or twice a month, not because that is an efficient way for them to run their business but because they feel it gives them greater control over their cash flow. They can tell a vendor that they will print their check at the first opportunity—which will be in two or three weeks in the very next check run. Unfortunately for them, this excuse often ends up with the vendor threatening to put the company on credit hold, which in turn results in manual Rush (and very inefficient) checks. As those familiar with the implications of Rush checks are well aware, this can in turn lead to an increase in duplicate payments and potential fraud.

Obviously, the size of the company and the number of checks it needs to issue will directly affect the frequency of its check runs.

Best Practices

Some might argue that the best practice when it comes to printing checks would be to not print any checks at all—to convert to a 100 percent electronic medium relying on the automated clearinghouse (ACH). They would probably be right. At this time, however attractive that proposition might be, this is not a reasonable approach. Given that fact, we'll take a look at the state of check printing today.

Regardless of the type of printing used (mainframe or laser), AP departments should make sure all affected parties know not only what their check run schedule is but also the cutoff points. If an approved invoice or check request needs to be received in AP by noon on Thursday in order to be included in a Friday check run, this vital information should be shared. Otherwise, people will show up in AP on Friday morning with requests, expecting them to be included in that day's check run. In the long run, it is far better to spend the time communicating this information (verbally, in writing, and on the department's intranet site) with everyone who could possibly be affected.

The process for printing checks in corporate America today is generally handled in one of two ways—either on a mainframe or on a laser printer. Best practices for printing on a mainframe will be discussed later in the chapter. Generally speaking, laser jet printers are now considered the ideal way to print checks, assuming appropriate safeguards are incorporated in the process. For starters, no check stock is required. The best practices for storing check stock are explained in the section under that heading. Some companies use numbered safety paper—a recommended best practice. This paper is numbered and incorporates many safety features. Each piece of paper is sequentially numbered.

A log is kept of the sequentially numbered safety paper. By itself, the paper is worthless. However, with the right software, it can be turned into a valuable commodity—a negotiable check. When it comes time to print checks, the number of checks to be printed should be calculated. The safety paper is removed from the secure location, the first number of the sequentially numbered paper noted, and the checks printed. The last number of the sequentially numbered paper is noted. A calculation should be made, based on the beginning number, the number of checks printed, the ending number, and any ruined sheets of paper, to ascertain that no additional checks were printed. It is especially important to collect any allegedly damaged paper and destroy it.

The number of people who can print checks should be kept to a minimum. The person who prints the checks, usually by controlling the software (through user IDs and passwords), should not have access to the check stock. Theoretically, when using a laser printer (which, by the way, are regular laser printers) a check run can be had any time a manual check is requested. Each company must make a determination of whether this is desirable and if it wishes to pursue that course.

When checks are printed this way, the process usually includes use of a facsimile signature. Typically, this signature is included on a separate plate. Companies take different stances on this plate—some leave them in the printer, while others remove them. If the plate is left in the printer (or is an integral part of the machine), additional care must be taken with the printer. It probably should not be left out on the open floor. Although it is true that in order to actually print a check someone would need access to the software and would need to have a password and user ID, a printer with a facsimile plate could turn a plain piece of paper into a negotiable check. (Remember, checks don't have to be printed on special safety paper, it's just a good idea.)

If preprinted check stock is used, a log similar to the one previously described should be kept. When it is time to run checks, one of the few approved staffers with access to the check stock closet should get the check stock out. Based on the number of checks that need to be run for each account, the appropriate number of checks should be removed. Some companies have so many different accounts that they end up using a cart to bring the appropriate number of checks for the different accounts to the computer room to be printed. The checks should not be stored in close proximity to the printer—it just makes it too easy for a thief. Typically, someone in Treasury or Accounting will bring the checks up to the Information Technology (IT) department to be run. This representative should watch while the checks are printed.

Since this type of check is typically of a continuous format, it is difficult, if not impossible, to rerun a check (in the same check run) if something goes wrong. When the checks are printed, notations should be made in the log regarding the first check number, the last check number, and the number of checks printed. Both the representative from Accounting (or Treasury) and IT should initial the log.

If a check prints off center, jams, or has some other problem, it should be voided—either by writing VOID across the check in capital letters or by tearing off the MICR (magnetic ink character recognition) line. In any event, all damaged checks should be kept after voiding them. This is to ensure that the checks are actually voided and do not land in the hands of a crook. Also, make sure the appropriate entries are made to your accounting logs or it will look like an uncashed check that should be turned over to the state as unclaimed property.

Some companies like to have two people present when checks are printed regardless of the methodology. In this case, both should calculate the number of checks used versus the check numbers and initial the log.

Periodically, the log used to verify check counts versus check paper used should be audited—and occasionally on a surprise basis.

At regular intervals, say once every two years, or if there is any significant change in activity (e.g., due to a merger or spin-off), a review of the frequency of check runs should be undertaken. As part of this process, an analysis of the number of rush checks (and the reasons for those requests) should be included. If too many rush checks are required, a company may want to increase the frequency of its check-printing process. In the upcoming years, if electronic payments continue to increase, many midsize companies may be able to cut back on the number of check runs they have each month.

Anyone involved in the check-printing process should have no responsibility for reconciling the company's bank accounts.

Once the checks are printed, they should be kept with great care until they are mailed. This means that if they are not mailed the same day they are printed (as they ideally should be), they need to be kept in a secure location. They should not be kept on the credenza of an executive who has to provide a second signature nor lying around the Accounts Payable department. More than one sticky-fingered employee or cleaning person has walked off with a check that did not belong to him or her.

Almost Best Practices

As you can see, especially if preprinted check stock is used, check printing can be a non–value-added, time-intensive task. Some companies choose to outsource this function to their banks. It adds little value and can cause a lot of trouble if not handled correctly.

Some would argue that including any check-printing data about anything other than laser printers in the "Best Practices" section is not appropriate and that printing continuous formatted checks on mainframes is not best practice. They might be correct. However, numerous companies still use continuous formatted checks, so they will be included in that section—at least for this edition of the book.

Reality Check for Accounts Payable

With a little bit of luck (okay, maybe a lot of luck) the check-printing function will diminish. For the last few years, the number of checks written has actually decreased. That decrease, at least for the titans of industry, has come through two best practices:

1. The use of purchase cards (p-cards) and other practices to eliminate small-dollar invoices from the corporate landscape

2. The move toward electronic payments primarily through the ACH

Thus, check printing may become less of a problem in the upcoming years.

Worst Practices

Worst practices include not taking the appropriate steps to guard both the check stock and the check-printing equipment. Several years ago an auditor noticed that his client had left the check-printing machine out in the open with the signature plate in the machine. Luckily for his client, he was an honest man. To make his point, he printed a check for $1 million made out to himself and left it on the controller's desk with a little note. The controller got the message and made the appropriate changes in the check-printing policies and procedures. Most importantly, a company that does not exercise "reasonable care" in its check-printing procedures could open itself up to incur all losses associated with any check fraud. The worst practices include

- Inappropriate segregation of duties
- Not exercising reasonable care in the check-printing process
- Not maintaining a log to count the number of checks printed versus authorized
- Not storing printed checks carefully before mailing

CHECK SIGNING

Background

As part of the bill-paying process, checks must be signed. How this is done should depend largely on the up-front controls used to vet the invoice and the approval process. In reality, there is a second component—corporate culture. In theory, if up-front controls for approvals and duplicate-payment checking were perfect, there would be no need for a check to be signed by anything other than a machine. Very few companies, unfortunately, are in a position or are willing to let every payment fly through the invoice-processing cycle without some level of senior management checking for high-dollar invoices. The definition of high-dollar invoice varies from company to company.

The information in this section assumes that the company is not using the check-signing process as a checkpoint to catch duplicate and inappropriate/unauthorized payments. If this is the case—and it is a really poor idea—then the company would not want to institute the practices designated in the "Best Practices" section but perhaps some hybrid as defined in the "Almost Best Practices" section.

The Board of Directors should authorize check signers. Alternatively, a senior-level executive who has been delegated by the Board may give others signatory responsibilities. In either event, banks will require signature cards so that they can verify signatures on checks presented for payment. Do not assume from a bank's request for signature cards that it is checking signatures. *Banks do not verify signatures.* Occasionally, they will spot check the signature on a check or pull a very-large-dollar check to verify the signature. The emphasis here is on the word *occasionally.* Any company that is counting on its bank to catch fraudulent checks will find itself with a load of bad checks unless it is using positive pay, which is discussed later in this chapter.

Best Practices

Most companies put their top-level executives, such as the chief executive officer (CEO), chief financial officer (CFO), and so on, on their bank accounts as signers, even though these individuals rarely sign checks. When these officers sign the annual report, they should *never* use their actual signature. This is for the company's protection and the protection of the officers personally. In the early days of check fraud, thieves simply got a copy of the company's annual report to get a legitimate signature to use in their crooked check activities. Since these executives rarely sign checks, it is recommended that they not be included as signers on bank accounts.

The selection of signers should depend on the number of checks that are manually signed as well as the personnel that will be available to actually sign the checks. Signers, however, should be of sufficient stature within the company and should check the documentation that accompanies the check for signature.

Most companies today use a mechanized check-signing procedure that is integrated with the check-printing cycle. Depending on the dollar amount of the check, the mechanized signature can be the only signature or the first signature. If a mechanized process is used, the signature plate needs to be maintained with proper care and controls. This means it should be easily separated from the machine (computer) that prints the check, or, if it is not removed, the check-printing computer should be kept in a secure location with controlled access. The signature plate, or the machine with the plate in it, needs to be kept in a secure location with limited access. Many companies keep the signature plate used for facsimile signatures in a safe.

Even if up-front controls are airtight, most companies will require two signatures on checks over a certain level. The level will depend on the nature of the business and corporate culture. A smaller company might require the second signature for all checks over $25,000, while a *Fortune* 500 company might set that level at $1 million. The level reflects the company's comfort level with its invoice-processing controls.

There is a lot of debate over whether a warning should be printed on the checks indicating the level where two signatures are required. This is similar to the warning regarding the maximum dollar amount for which a check can be written. Some believe that putting a notice on the check stating "Checks over $25,000 require two signatures" is a good idea as it alerts the teller to a possible fraud. Others rightly note that such an indicator is likely to be of more use to a crook than to the teller. A crook noting such a warning will simply alter the check to no more than $24,999.

Most AP and Treasury groups at large companies keep a list of bank accounts and authorized signers. This is a good idea as long as proper care is taken with these reports. They should be limited in number and given only to those employees who need the information—definitely a need-to-know report. When the report is updated, the old reports should be collected and destroyed. Employees who receive the report should keep it in their desks, not lying on top for easy access.

In no case should anyone who is an authorized signer on any account do bank account reconciliations.

When manual signatures are used on checks, the responsibility for getting the signatures (a truly thankless task) should be given to someone other than the person who prepares the checks.

When the check is given to the signer for signature, all the appropriate backup should be attached and the signer should verify that

- The check is actually for the invoices presented.
- The appropriate approvals are in place.
- The check is drawn on the correct account.
- The check is for the correct amount.

If the signer is not willing or capable of this verification process, he or she should not be an authorized signer.

Periodically, spot check checks automatically signed to verify quality control.

Almost Best Practices

When companies are not comfortable without a senior review of most outgoing checks, the level where automated signing is acceptable is usually set quite low. Rather than fighting City Hall, AP can suggest that the level be gradually raised. As comfort is gained, the levels can be periodically raised.

Another way to address the issue of having too many checks is to look for ways to eliminate checks, especially checks for low-dollar purchases. Use of p-cards, electronic payments through the ACH, and direct deposit for travel and entertainment (T&E) reimbursements will help address the issue.

Reality Check for Accounts Payable

Despite their best intentions, few authorized signers will actually go through the appropriate verification process before signing a check. The bulk of the responsibility for those tasks still lies with the AP staff, and if there is an error, it is rarely the signer who is held responsible.

Worst Practices

Worst practices include

- *Signing checks with a rubber stamp.* Although the ease with which checks can be signed with a rubber stamp is appealing to many, it has serious drawbacks. It is so easy for a thief to copy a signature made with a rubber stamp that a company that uses a rubber stamp to sign its checks is *not* considered to be using ordinary care. The implications of not using ordinary care mean that should any check fraud happen, the company would be liable for 100 percent of the loss.

- *Some companies, thinking they are improving controls, set the dollar level at which hand signatures are required very low.* When an executive is presented with many checks to sign at one time, it is unlikely that he will give each an adequate review. Rather than set the dollar level low, it is far better to set it higher, have fewer checks representing higher dollar invoices undergo a thorough review.

CHECK STOCK STORAGE

Background

Blank checks may look innocuous enough, but in the wrong hands they can cause a lot of damage. A thief, disgruntled employee, or even just an inexperienced staffer can cause untold trouble by misusing company checks. In the past, banks ate the losses associated with check fraud. This is no longer the case. They just can't afford these hits to their bottom line. Often, this is an area that is overlooked—no one gives it much thought. However, with all the attention of the recent accounting scandals, the enactment of the Sarbanes-Oxley Act, and the new emphasis on internal controls, how a company stores its checks is likely to come under increased scrutiny.

Best Practices

In the "Check Printing" section, there was a discussion of both laser checks printed on safety paper and preprinted checks. While this discussion does cover both types, it applies to preprinted checks to a larger degree, as that is where the real risk lies.

- Checks should be stored in a secure, locked location.

- Access to the check stock should be severely limited.
- The closet should be reinforced—and not of the type that a crook could easily hack into.
- The lock on the door should be substantial and not easily picked with a hairpin or clothes hanger.

Ideally, the check storage closet should not be in close proximity to the printer. If someone breaks in, especially on a long weekend, don't make it too easy for him or her.

Sufficient segregation of duties should be incorporated into the various tasks associated with the check production cycle, so the individuals with access to the check storage closet do not also have the authority to print checks. Clearly, anyone with access to the check storage closet should not be responsible for the reconciliation of the company's bank accounts.

Almost Best Practices

When it comes to storing of checks, there is not much give and take. It is something that a company really needs to do right—the consequences of doing it wrong are too great.

Reality Check for Accounts Payable

The check stock storage issue is likely to be a touchy issue at some smaller midsize companies. If the check stock or a spare checkbook has always been kept in the assistant controller's office, he or she may be insulted at the suggestion that it really should be moved to a more secure location.

Worst Practices

Worst practices include

- Keeping a spare checkbook around, in someone's desk, for those after-hour emergency situations

41

- Keeping checks in the bottom drawer of a filing cabinet, especially if that cabinet is often open and unattended for long periods of time
- Storing the check printer (and signature plate) in the same locked room as the check stock
- Not adequately segregating duties when it comes to check printing, storage, and the reconciliation of bank accounts

DISTRIBUTION OF CHECKS

Background

Once a check is printed and signed, it has to get in the hands of the payee. The normal way that this is handled is to mail the check to the payee. In fact, some may wonder why there is a separate section for this topic. The answer is that sometimes the person requesting the check will request that the check be returned to him or her for final distribution. Typically, there are three semi-legitimate reasons that this request is made:

1. The requestor wants to make sure that the check is mailed correctly.
2. The requestor is a salesperson who wants to deliver the check to the customer and try and pick up another order at the same time.
3. The requestor has some other business relationship with the payee and wants to solidify that relationship.

While the reasons may appear reasonable at first glance, they are overridden by several other concerns, including the following:

- It is extremely inefficient and time consuming to return checks to the requestor. Few people outside Accounts Payable realize how disruptive the practice is.

- The door for employee fraud is opened wide whenever checks are returned to anyone other than the payee.
- Checks returned to the requestors are sometimes lost, misplaced, or not delivered for a long time, often resulting in duplicate payments.

Best Practices

When an invoice is approved for payment, the invoice should have a mailing address on it. Additionally, this address should match the Pay-To address in the master vendor file. Any variation from this should be investigated because it may be the first sign that something is amiss. Under all but the most extenuating circumstances, checks should be mailed.

When checks are mailed, care should be taken regarding when and how this is done. Checks should be sealed in envelopes and delivered either straight to the post office or to the mailroom at the end of the day.

If checks are delivered to the mailroom, they should not be left out in the open where anyone walking by can see them and easily filch one. This is especially true if temporary employees are frequently used.

Similarly, thought should be given as to whether a window envelope should be used. While window envelopes simplify the mailing of checks, they are also a red flag for a crook looking for checks to steal. Rarely are checks mailed in anything other than window envelopes.

Additionally, if one-part sealers (those multipart forms that contain the check) are used, extra care should be taken in the mailing procedures. Again, they are often a red flag to crooks looking for checks.

Almost Best Practices

Sometimes, either the corporate culture or the nature of the business will require the hand delivery of checks, either to company employees or to the customers' representatives. In these cases, to avoid disrupting the AP department too much, the pickup time should be limited to certain days and hours.

A log should be kept for checks not mailed. Each time a check is picked up, the following information should be noted in the log:

- Check number
- Payee
- Dollar amount
- Date the check was issued
- Date the check was picked up
- Name of the person picking the check up

The person picking the check up should sign each of the entries. Of course, the list of who can pick up checks should also be limited.

Although companies often tolerate the practice of not mailing checks directly to the payee, it should be discouraged. Anytime someone requests that a check be returned, ask why he or she needs it and then point out the advantages of not returning the check.

Paying customers electronically eliminates this issue!

Reality Check for Accounts Payable

If the company tolerates the practice of individuals picking up checks, there will be occasions when AP will have to make these checks available outside of the preset hours. This practice should be discouraged as much as possible.

If checks are to be regularly segregated for delivery rather than mailing, firm policies and procedures should be written to govern the process.

Worst Practices

Worst practices include the returning of checks to anyone other than the payee, especially if the person who approved the invoice for payment is the individual to whom the check is returned.

Although circumstances may dictate the issuing of a manual check and returning it to the individual who approved the payment, these should be limited.

CHECK FRAUD

Background

Although no one knows the true level of check fraud, most experts estimate that it is at least a $10 billion-a-year business. In years gone by, banks would eat the losses associated with check fraud for their corporate clients. This has become prohibitively expensive, and banks are no longer willing or able to absorb these often unnecessary expenses. Changes to the Uniform Commercial Code (UCC) have introduced the concepts of *reasonable care* and *comparative culpability*. In plain English this means the person in the best position to prevent the crime will be held responsible. This is done on a pro-rata basis, although there are some things that companies do that place the responsibility 100 percent on their plate. A simple example of this is using a rubber stamp (not a facsimile signer) to sign checks and not keeping check stock in a secure location.

Those who are interested in reading the statutes that cover payment fraud–related issues can refer to

- UCC3 for ordinary care
- UCC4 for reasonable notification
- UCC4A for acceptable security procedures
- Regulation CC for shortened return/hold times

- The National Automated Clearing House Association (NACHA) for unauthorized entries return
- Certain state statutes

The states have also changed their laws so that companies that fail to exercise "reasonable care" are now allocated the losses associated with check fraud.

Best Practices

While at first blush making all payments electronically might seem to eliminate the problem, it is not practical in today's environment. Numerous companies are not able to take this step, and even more limiting is the fact that a number of their customers are not yet ready to accept payments electronically. Five years from now this might be an appropriate mechanism, depending on the evolution of the market.

A reasonable best practice for companies is to move as many of their customers to an electronic payment mechanism as possible. In most instances this will require a renegotiation of the payment terms to make the transaction float neutral. If a customer sees the move toward electronic payments as an attempt on the part of the vendor to improve its position, it is unlikely to agree to pay electronically. In a float-neutral situation, both parties still benefit from improved efficiencies and reduced costs.

A few years ago, the use of positive pay was seen as a leading-edge technique to limit check fraud. Today, it should be part of the payment process at every company. Some think that in a few short years not using positive pay will be seen as not exercising reasonable care. Positive pay is a service offered by most banks. As part of the service, companies transmit to their banks their check issuance file each time checks are written. The file contains a list of check numbers and dollar amounts. When a check is presented for payment, it is matched against the file. If there is a match, the check is honored and the check number removed from the file. It there is no match, the check is handled according to the preset instructions from the company. This may mean automatically rejecting the item, but more likely it means notifying the company and giving it a few hours to send instructions on how the item should be handled. What has been described so far is the basic positive pay service. New enhancements offered by some banks include

- Image positive pay
- Teller positive pay
- Payee name positive pay

Companies should contact their bankers for the details of the products offered.

In addition to positive pay, companies also need to focus on the check itself. The check should contain some (but not necessarily all) of the following security features:

- *Void pantographs.* A pantograph is a design that is not clearly visible until a copy has been made when such words as *VOID* or *COPY* become visible, making the copy non-negotiable
- *Watermarks.* Watermarks are subtle designs of a logo or other image. Designed to foil copiers and scanners that operate by imaging at right angles (90 degrees), watermarks are viewed by holding a check at a 45-degree angle.
- *Microprinting.* A word or a phrase is printed on the check so small that to the eye it appears as a solid line. When magnified or viewed closely, the word or phrase will become apparent. Copiers and scanners can't reproduce at this level of detail, so microprinting when copied will appear as a solid line.

- *Laid lines.* Laid lines are unevenly spaced lines that appear on the back of a check and are part of the check paper. This design makes it difficult to cut and paste information such as payee name and dollar amount without detection.
- *Reactive safety paper.* This paper combats erasure and chemical alteration by "bleeding" when a forger tries to erase or chemically alter information on the check, leaving the check discolored.
- *Special inks.* These are highly reactive inks that discolor when they come into contact with erasure chemical solvents.
- *Color prismatic printing.* This type of printing creates a multicolor pantograph background that is extremely difficult to duplicate when using a color copier or scanner.
- *Special borders.* These borders on the check have intricate designs that, if copied, become distorted images.
- *Warning bands.* Warning bands describe the security features present on a check. These bands alert bank tellers or store clerks to inspect the check before accepting it. They may also act as a deterrent to criminals.
- *Thermochromic inks.* These are special, colored inks that are sensitive to human touch and, when activated, either change color or disappear.
- *Toner grip.* This is a special coating on the check paper that provides maximum adhesion of the MICR toner to the check paper. This helps prevent the alteration of payee or dollar amount by making erasure or removal of information more difficult.

Checks should not be ordered from a printer but rather printed as needed. This means that all the controls surrounding check stock become irrelevant because the only thing the company has ordered is blank paper. The appropriate controls need to be with the software and hardware used to print the checks.

Almost Best Practices

Not every company is willing or able to walk away from preprinted check stock. If the company does use preprinted check stock, appropriate care must be taken to ensure that checks are stored under lock and key and access to the storage area is limited. Additionally, anyone who is an authorized signer or has access to the safe where the signature plates for the check-signing machine (or computer) are kept should not have access to the check stock.

While use of the basic positive pay service or one of the innovations, such as image positive pay, teller positive pay, or payee name positive pay, is definitely a best practice, some companies have trouble transmitting an issue tape to the bank. For these companies, reverse positive pay is a reasonable option, while they try and alleviate the situation that prevents them from giving the bank a check issuance tape. In this case the bank will transmit a file to the company containing all the checks clearing against the company's account that morning. The company is then responsible for reviewing the information within a few hours and contacting the bank about any that should not be honored. Alternatively, the company can make arrangements with the bank that it honor all checks unless notified.

Reality Check for Accounts Payable

Accounts Payable often has a hard time convincing management that positive pay should be used. Don't let this issue drop. Similarly, companies are often very attached to preprinted checks. Again, it is up to the AP executives at companies like this to make sure that adequate controls are used with regard to the check stock.

Worst Practices

Worst practices include

- Not using positive pay
- Not keeping checks in a secure location
- Not incorporating fraud prevention features in check stock
- Using a rubber stamp to sign checks

RUSH OR EMERGENCY CHECKS

Background

Rush checks, also referred to as emergency checks or ASAP checks, are the bane of many AP departments. They are traditionally manually written, although in recent years they have been printed by computers and are produced outside the normal check production cycle. They are supposed to be for those once-in-a-lifetime emergencies that crop up with varying frequency depending on the nature of the business and the tolerance of the corporation for this type of behavior. In reality, they are sometimes written to cover for the sloppy habits of certain employees, such as executives who get behind in their work and neglect to approve invoices for payment, harried purchasing managers who lose an invoice in the stacks of paper on their desk, or late-to-the-game employees who rush in an expense report the day their credit card bill is due.

The problem with these transactions is that an employee in the AP department is forced to stop his or her work to process the rush request. While everyone realizes that there are true emergencies, and invoices on rare occasions do get lost in the mail, the practice of relying on AP to bail out others for poor work habits comes at a cost that is much higher than it appears.

The hidden costs associated with these transactions include

- The AP associate must interrupt his or her work to process the request. If this happens more than very occasionally, an additional person will have to be added to the staff or overtime will be accrued.
- The person whose work was interrupted will have to find exactly where he or she was when work was stopped and continue. This increases the chances of an error that will have to be corrected at a later point.
- Manual checks will have to be entered in the system to get onto the company's books at a later point, taking more time. If the company is using positive pay, the check issuance file that is given to the bank has to be adjusted.
- Duplicate payment audit firms report that there is an increased risk for a duplicate payment anytime a check is written outside the normal cycle. The cost of recovering duplicate payments is huge.

There is one other consideration when it comes to rush checks. There is also an increased risk of check fraud with rush checks, especially if they are used often and the check issuance files given to the bank for positive pay are sloppily updated.

Best Practices

By now you probably realize that the very best practice when it comes to rush checks is to "just say no" and never issue checks outside the normal check production cycle.

Almost Best Practices

The harsh reality is that few companies can afford to take such a harsh stance. Nor are many senior management teams willing to back such a practice. Few AP associates are willing to tell the secretary of the president of the company that a check will not be issued for the president, regardless of the reason. A more reasoned approach is to issue Rush checks occasionally under very strict guidelines. These might include requiring

- Very-senior-level authorization so that the employees understand that it is a process for only true emergencies and so management begins to understand the level of discomfort these transactions cause. More than one senior manager has reported that she thought AP was making a big deal out of nothing regarding Rush checks. After having their work interrupted several times a day, senior managers often quickly change their opinion.

- The person making the request to get the senior-level approval. This often makes the requester think twice about whether or not the emergency is really an emergency.

- A thorough checking of the files before the Rush check is issued. Sometimes, requestors find that the payment the vendor claimed it didn't receive was in fact deposited at the vendor's lockbox and the cash applied incorrectly.

- That AP thoroughly question the requestor about the reasons for the rush request as well as the date when the payment must be made. Often, these requests are made out of ignorance about the actual AP procedures, and with a little investigation it will turn out that the request can be handled through the normal cycle.

- That AP keep a file with copies of all the rush check requests in it. Since most times when a duplicate payment occurs that is related to a rush request and a lost invoice, it is the original invoice that gets paid the second time—not the second request invoice. Eventually, the original invoice, whether it was lost in the mail or on someone's desk, finds its way to AP and is paid. If the number of Rush checks issued is small, as it should be, the file will be thin. Once a month, an associate in the AP department should check to ensure that the rush invoices were not paid a second time. If such a payment is discovered, the company can work with the supplier to recover the payment rather than paying its duplicate payment audit firm to handle the task.

Additionally, AP managers might

- Prepare a monthly report for senior management showing the number of rush requests by requestor. After a while, if management backs AP, no one will want to be on the top of this report.
- Even if management is not overly supportive of reducing the number of rush checks, keep track of the most frequent requestors, payees, and causes for these requests. Then work with the offending parties and the company's purchase-to-pay procedures to close any loopholes that might be causing these requests. Sometimes the root cause can be quite simple. For example, if invoices are arriving very late, look at the Bill-To address. Is it correct? Is the invoice being addressed to the right party or is it floating around the company before eventually landing on the right desk?
- Make sure everyone who requests payments is aware of the check production schedule. This includes letting them know what the cutoff dates are for each check run.
- Periodically, review its procedures and its check run schedule to see if they have sufficient controls and are adequate to meet the company's needs.

Reality Check for Accounts Payable

While the AP department is well aware of the problems associated with Rush checks, AP managers also need to be aware of the corporate culture within their own organization. If the Purchasing manager asks for a Rush check and AP refuses, he or she is likely to go over their heads. It is imperative that AP has a good read on how management will react. If 95 times out of 100 it will back the Purchasing manager, then AP managers are advised to avoid the confrontation, grit their teeth, and find ways to work with Purchasing to reduce the number of these incidents.

Worst Practices

Unfortunately, when it comes to rush or emergency payments, many terrible practices are in use today. They include, but are not limited to

- Issuing manual checks whenever anyone asks
- Requiring little or no documentation proving that the rush request has not already been honored
- Not checking for duplicate payments

CASE STUDY

Information Sheet:
Segregation of Duties

One of the themes that runs through this book involves the discussion of checks and balances and the segregation of duties. While at a large company it is very easy to ensure that no one individual is in a position to defraud the company, it is more difficult at companies with smaller accounting/AP staffs. Typically, it is recommended that no individual have the authority to do more than one of the following:

- Ordering check stock
- Storing check stock
- Printing checks
- Mailing checks
- Approving invoices for payment
- Signing checks
- Entering vendor information in the master vendor file
- Setting up new accounts in the master vendor file
- Reconciliation of company's bank accounts

Someone who signs checks might also occasionally approve invoices for payment. Ideally, someone else should sign the checks for any invoices this individual may have approved. In the real world, this rarely happens.

In light of the increased scrutiny on internal controls as a result of the Sarbanes-Oxley legislation, companies are starting to review their segregation of duties. Those who have not done this in a long time can take a look at how they are set up and adjust. In reality, many companies automatically put numerous high-level executives on as bank account signers and invoice approvers and occasionally provide some of them (most typically the controller, treasurer, and/or CFO) with access to the check storage closet, the signature plate, and so on. This is not really a good idea. Let's face it—the CFO is unlikely to ever get checks out of the closet, so why give him or her access?

3

Operational

Running an Accounts Payable (AP) department is full of details. In addition to the wide array of tasks that must be done each day, there are some operational issues that should be addressed to keep the department running smoothly. In this chapter, we'll look at

- Duplicate payment avoidance
- Paying when the original invoice is missing
- Limiting the calls into AP
- Petty cash
- Statements

DUPLICATE PAYMENT AVOIDANCE

Background

One of the dirty little secrets in the corporate world is the fact that companies regularly pay a certain small percentage of their invoices more than once. This occurs at even the most well-run companies. Many recognize the fact that, even with the most stringent controls and technology, duplicate payments do slip through. This can occur when

- Invoices get lost in the mail
- Invoices sit on an approver's desk for weeks
- Companies decide to stretch terms and the supplier sends a second invoice because it did not get paid
- Rush or manual checks are used
- Fraud—both vendor and employee
- Disputes are not resolved in a timely manner
- A myriad of other factors

An unfortunate part of the duplicate payment issue is the large number of companies that truly believe they never make a duplicate payment. While their processes may be first class, mistakes happen. Additionally, fraud happens and the crooks who perpetrate invoice fraud know about duplicate payment checks—and they also know how to circumvent them.

The companies that believe they never make duplicate payments are often reluctant to bring in a duplicate payment audit firm. This is false vanity. Another reason some companies object to duplicate payment audit firms is that they think they are too expensive. However, because most of these firms work on an incentive basis, earning a percentage of what they find, bringing one in costs nothing. With an audit firm, at least the company collects a percentage of the duplicate payment; without it, the company collects nothing.

Best Practices

For starters, companies need to recognize that duplicate payments can and will occur, and they need to continually guard against it by

- Implementing best practices around the master vendor file (see Chapter 4)

- Insisting that approvals on invoices be done in a timely manner (see "Invoice Handling: Approvals" section in Chapter 1)
- Establishing some simple routines, such as running invoice numbers against dollar amounts to quickly identify obvious duplicates
- Minimizing the number of manual checks written
- Setting up a policy for consistently creating invoice numbers for invoices without invoice numbers. The guidelines should include rules for logically creating invoice numbers. All personnel should be instructed on the invoice numbering protocol.
- Establishing a policy when paying from copies rather than original invoices
- Bringing in an outside audit firm. Not only will they recover the duplicate payments that were made in the past, but they will identify the holes in your procedures—loopholes that you can close so that duplicate payments in the future will be minimized. Many firms believe that they do not make duplicate payments and therefore do not need to bring in an outside audit firm.
- Insisting that the duplicate payment audit firm not only recover funds, but also identify procedural weak spots in your organization. The firms should also make recommendations as to what the company can do to tighten its policies and procedures.

Almost Best Practices

By identifying a critical dollar level, say $100,000 or perhaps $25,000, companies can take a huge bite out of the duplicate payment problem by routinely double checking these larger payments to ensure that a duplicate payment is not being made.

Each time a duplicate payment is identified, review the paperwork to see if you can identify the root cause. Once that cause has been identified, work to eliminate the problem.

If certain vendors tend to have duplicate payments more frequently than others, routinely double check all transactions with that vendor. Similarly, if a certain approver tends to be associated with more duplicate payments, work with that approver.

Reality Check for Accounts Payable

Duplicate payments will happen, regardless of how tight the controls are. Accounts Payable is often concerned that it will be blamed for any duplicate payments. That happens occasionally, although it is usually unfair. More often, it provides AP with the ammunition needed to get the changes it wants implemented. Too often, AP knows that processes should be changed or improved but it cannot get the resources or support needed to implement those changes. The recommendations from the audit firm are often the turning point that gets management moving.

There is another untold tale related to duplicate payment audit firms. Some of them report that they go back to the same companies year after year, finding the same type of duplicate payments over and over again. It's not that the audit firm hasn't given recommendations for change—the company has just not implemented them.

Worst Practices

Worst practices include

- Relying on the "memory" of the AP associate to identify duplicate payments. This is an atrocious practice that is unfair to the AP associate, but it is still used at some companies.

- Having no duplicate payment checks in your process
- Not implementing any of the recommendations made by the duplicate payment audit firm
- Not using an outside audit firm to check for duplicate payments

PAYING WHEN THE ORIGINAL INVOICE IS MISSING

Background

We all know of instances in which the U.S. mail delivered letters or cards weeks or even months late. Even in the most efficient organizations, papers, including invoices, do get lost.

Best Practices

Obviously, the best control of never paying from a copy is not realistic in most cases. Telling the utility company or a valued supplier that you do not pay unless you have the original invoice is likely to bring about undesirable consequences, that is, no electricity or being put on credit hold and not being able to get needed supplies—something management at most companies would not find acceptable.

Almost Best Practices

The next step is to make it difficult for those who try to pay from copies. Why? Some people would much rather call the vendor and ask that another copy of the invoice be faxed over rather than actually sort through their desk to find the missing invoice. The AP associate, with management's approval, needs to make it easier to look for the invoice than to get it paid from a copy. This can be done by

- Requiring two or more additional signatures from higher-level employees on copies of invoices, say the requestor's supervisor and the controller
- Paying from a copy only after the invoice is 30 or 60 days old
- Requiring that a manual search of the files be made to ensure the invoice was already paid
- Holding on to the invoice for an additional five to seven days to see if the original "mysteriously" appears. You'll be surprised how often this happens.
- Double checking the file to make sure that the payment was not already made
- If Purchasing made the request, demanding that a valid PO and an unmatched receiver be provided
- Making sure the duplicate is marked "Copy" and filed immediately
- Running the information through a search routine based on the invoice number and dollar amount
- Requiring an explanation for the lack of an original invoice with the payment request
- Reviewing requests for payment without an original invoice and making a determination on a case-by-case basis as to the advisability of paying. Be sure to get your manager's input before rejecting a request.
- Having the request for payment signed by the individual who has the primary relationship with the vendor
- Paying from a copy only if the invoice number is completely legible. If not, ask for a clean copy so that you can check against invoice number.

Reality Check for Accounts Payable

Marking the second invoice as a copy or stamping it "Duplicate" does not really help when the original invoice shows up.

Unless an extensive search is made of the files, it is unlikely that this action will help.

Worst Practices

Worst practices include having no policy about paying when the original invoice is missing.

LIMITING CALLS TO ACCOUNTS PAYABLE

Background

Most AP professionals can be quite efficient if given the chance. However, with the phone constantly ringing, it is hard to get any work done. Yet, there is not much of an alternative—people (both vendors and other employees) need information.

Best Practices

There are two issues with the calls to AP. First, it is necessary to find a way to answer the legitimate inquiries that come through the department. Second, AP needs to find efficient ways to get information in the hands of those who need it.

There are several ways to efficiently answer legitimate inquiries, including

- Setting up a help line and staffing it with one or more customer service–oriented employees
- Setting up an e-mail address to answer vendor and/or employee inquiries. Make sure the responses go out within 48 hours.
- Setting aside a few hours each day to answer inquiries. Let vendors and employees know this time.

One of the best ways to address vendors' need for payment and invoice status information is through use of a password-protected Internet site or interactive voice response (IVR). For additional information on these two approaches, see Chapter 10.

The time spent answering inquiries can be reduced if information is shared with vendors and employees in other ways. The AP department should have either its own Web site or several pages on the company's site. Information for employees that is covered on an intranet should include

- Answers to frequently asked AP questions
- AP contact list, with phone extensions and responsibilities
- AP deadlines for check requests
- AP policy and procedures manual
- Travel and entertainment (T&E) policy and forms
- Petty cash policy and forms
- Purchasing card (p-card) information
- All other AP forms
- Copies of past issues of your internal AP newsletter, if there is one

For vendors, the company's Internet site should include the following information:

- Payment status of open invoices
- AP contact list, with phone numbers and responsibilities
- Company's invoice and supplier policies
- Company's W-9 policy for independent contractors

Whenever there is a change to policy or procedures, information should be communicated via a memo or e-mail and posted on the appropriate intranet/Internet site.

Almost Best Practices

Almost best practices include establishing guidelines for the types of questions that AP will answer. For example, some AP departments refuse to investigate a missing payment until the invoice is more than 30 days past due. While this might be efficient for the AP department, it is poor from a vendor relations standpoint.

Reality Check for Accounts Payable

Accept the fact that no matter how good the AP department's policies and procedures are, there will be interruptions. The goal is simply to minimize these disruptions.

Worst Practices

Worst practices include having no policy or procedure for answering vendor inquiries and simply hoping for the best.

PETTY CASH

Background

Traditionally, companies have utilized petty cash boxes to pay for small-dollar charges that arise in the day-to-day running of the business. Ideally, the box would have a small amount of cash in it and employees would be reimbursed for approved purchases. They would have a receipt of some sort or a form signed by an authorized approver. The petty cash box would be kept locked in a safe. Ideally, the person with the key to the box would be a different individual than the person who knew the combination of the safe.

Some companies took the "petty cash" box to new levels, using it to advance funds to executives taking clients out for lunch or dinner. This was before T&E cards, so this use is really no longer valid.

Companies wanting to make the lives of their executives a little easier would also sometimes cash personal checks in the petty cash box. Again, this was before the days of 24-hour automated teller machines (ATMs). The convenience factor has diminished greatly.

At some companies, not only would the checks of high-level executives be cashed, but employees running the box would cash checks for other employees as well.

In some companies the petty cash function will reside in Treasury and in others in the AP department. Regardless of where the function lies, very stringent guidelines should be adhered to when maintaining the function.

The opportunity for abuse and outright fraud is huge. Phony receipts, questionable accounting, and no real review of the funds spent are just a few of the problems. At a large company, where spending is scrutinized closely, extensive use of petty cash throws the analysis off. One company, after eliminating petty cash, discovered it spent $50,000 a year on pizza for employees working late. Armed with this information, it was able to negotiate a slightly better price on orders. Still another discovered that many of its regional locations were sending flowers to employees to celebrate certain life events (e.g., weddings, births, deaths). There was no uniformity: One location might send a $50 bouquet, while another would send a $150 arrangement for the same event.

Best Practices

Don't have a petty cash box. They are extremely inefficient and leave the door wide open to petty fraud. Given the wide variety of alternatives available today, there is no need for petty cash. Instead, companies can

- Encourage executives and managers to use their p-cards or T&E cards to pay for the item in question.
- Pay for the items themselves and put in for reimbursement on their expense reports.

- If a lower-level employee is involved, the department manager can pay for the item and put in for reimbursement on an expense report.
- Have the vendor bill for the item.

Almost Best Practices

If the company insists on a petty cash box, and in some circumstances corporate culture might dictate one, limit its use. While it might not be the best use of the AP department's time and resources, if management decrees that there should be a petty cash box, AP will have to run it. Similarly, if management wants executives' personal checks cashed, again, AP will have to cash the checks. The following can be done to keep the petty cash function under control:

- Have a written policy delineating the use of the box
- Limit the access to the box.
- Keep a log of who goes into the box, the beginning balance, all withdrawals, and the ending balance. Ideally, two individuals should verify these items and initial the log.
- Internal audit should perform unscheduled audits of the box.
- Limit the time when the box is open. Don't reimburse employees whenever they show up (unless, of course, it is a true emergency). If possible, open the box only once a week to reimburse employees.
- Whenever a reimbursement is requested, look for other ways to handle the charge. Even if the employee is paid, point out ways the matter could be addressed in the future without resorting to petty cash.
- Never, under any circumstances, take an IOU in the petty cash box.

- Never reimburse an employee who does not have proper documentation and authorization for the expense.
- Replenish the box on a timely basis. Don't allow the box to run low on cash.
- Set stringent checks on who can take money in and out of the box. With several hands in the pot, it can get ugly if money is missing.
- Publish a schedule, along with the requirements for reimbursement, and share it with all employees likely to use the box.
- Periodically, review the expenses reimbursed from the box and look for alternative ways to pay for those expenses.

Any AP department that runs a petty cash box should document the amount of time that it spends running and maintaining the box. Calculate the cost and the number of person-hours devoted to the task, and try and use this information to either eliminate the box or at least minimize the items that can be cashed in the box.

Reality Check for Accounts Payable

No matter how hard you push for the elimination of a petty cash box, there are companies, because of corporate culture or specialized industry practices, that will insist on having one. There are times when you just can't fight City Hall. When this happens, just try and make it as nonintrusive as possible.

Worst Practices

There are many worst practices. Lax controls surrounding the storage of the box, access to the box, reimbursement documentation, and the timing of reimbursements can lead to losses and inefficiencies in the AP department. Some of the worst practices include:

- Acceptance of IOUs from employees running a little short on cash
- Use of the cash in the box in anticipation of management's approving an expenditure
- Acceptance and cashing of a postdated check

SUPPLIER STATEMENTS

Background

Some suppliers will send their customers a monthly statement showing unpaid outstanding invoices. These monthly reports can be of great assistance if used correctly, or can lead to disaster if not. What AP managers and other professionals need to be aware of is that many vendors will send statements showing outstanding invoices only. They will not include any of the outstanding credits. When the customer is kept in the dark about outstanding credits, it makes it very difficult for the customer to take the credit.

Best Practices

Accounts Payable should ask every supplier for a statement each month or each quarter. When this request is made, it should be made very clear to the vendor that you want *all* activity reflected on that statement. Without that demand, the credits will not be included on many statements.

When the statements are received they should be reviewed—*not* with an eye to making payments but in order to identify outstanding invoices that have not been received and credits. This information should be used to either take the credits or initiate a search for the missing invoices. In no case should payments be made on the basis of a statement that reflects a missing invoice. In fact, with one main exception, statements should never be used in place of an invoice for payment purposes. One of the leading causes of duplicate payments is making payments from both statements and the original invoice.

The exception regarding making payments from statements has to do with vendors that send numerous small-dollar invoices, for example, for overnight delivery services or temp help. Arrangements can be made with these vendors to pay them once a week or once a month based on the statement rather than individual invoices. However, once these arrangements have been made with a vendor, payments should never be made from an invoice. The policy should limit to one type. Occasionally, a vendor will not be able to suppress the printing of invoices, and they will end up in AP. Therefore, you cannot trust the supplier not to send the invoice, so the policy and procedures of the firm should address this issue.

Almost Best Practices

An overworked AP department may not have the time to review statements on a monthly basis. In any event, statements should be requested and reviewed at least once a year. This can be done during the AP slow period, that is, not the end of the month, beginning of the month, end of the year, January, tax time, and so on.

Reality Check for Accounts Payable

When a vendor sends in a statement and it appears to be accurate, don't stop there. Don't take the vendor's word. Double check to make sure that the vendor has included all activity and credits.

Worst Practices

Worst practices include

- Paying from statements when there is no agreement with the supplier that the statement will be used for payment purposes—in place of individual invoices. Probably one of the worst approaches, because it leads to an incredible number of duplicate payments, is the practice of noticing a severely delinquent invoice on a statement and paying it. Eventually, that tardy invoice will find its way down to AP with an approval on it, and it will be paid a second time!

- Paying the same vendor from both statements and invoices

- Paying credits. Yes, there are a few novice AP professionals who don't understand that credits are money owed to the firm, not by the firm. They go ahead and pay the credit, doubling the money now owed the company.

CASE STUDY

Expert Demonstrates How to Put the Web to Work for Accounts Payable

We've all heard the expression, "Don't work harder, work smarter." Companies everywhere are starting to implement that approach by taking advantage of the Internet to control areas such as invoice handling, T&E, and procurement. Speaking at a recent conference, Charles Schwab's vice president, Sandy Campos, explained how her company harnessed the power of the Web to achieve these goals.

BACKGROUND

"Just when you think you understand the game," began Campos, "somebody changes the rules." That's certainly the way it's been in Accounts Payable at Schwab over the last few years. She said that Schwab experienced tremendous growth in the last five years of the 1990s. The firm's operational and administrative functions struggled to keep pace with the growth, utilizing the obvious strategy: It hired more people to handle the ever-growing transaction volume. Then one day a light went on. The firm realized that just hiring more people was not an effective long-term prescription to address the corporate growing pains.

Schwab needed to free up people to focus on the core business. Campos says that the way the company is doing this is by creating a self-service environment, which offers streamlined, paperless, seamless, online access to information. While this sounds wonderful in theory, how can Accounts Payable departments achieve this goal?

GETTING STARTED

It wasn't difficult to identify the processes that were ripe for improvement. Campos says the company decided to focus on processes that were in support of employee and third-party self-service, manually intensive, and repetitious in nature. Processes that were also ripe for improvement were those that were challenging to control, time consuming, managed by several organizations, paper based, and geographically dispersed.

With so many areas fitting these descriptions, the difficult part was to identify those AP functions that did not meet the criteria.

GOALS

Schwab wanted to achieve three specific goals in AP:

1. *Cycle time.* The company wanted faster processing, the elimination of duplicate data entry, and the reduction of errors. Additionally, it wanted online update and edit capabilities and workflow.

2. *Information availability.* Ideally, the company strove to have real-time access to current information, to reduce printing and distribution costs, and to eliminate paper.

3. *Process controls.* The company wanted to enforce requirements and standards and to automate the audit process by applying defined business rules and policies.

WHAT SCHWAB HAS ACCOMPLISHED

The company implemented a number of electronic initiatives, including

- *eT&E.* Replacing the paper reimbursement forms that had to be completed and mailed to AP for manual data input and payment processing was an e-mail–based T&E application (eT&E). It is routed electronically for approval, processing, and payment. Reimbursement now occurs in two to three days instead of two to three weeks.

- *Invoice handling.* Invoices are scanned to create a digital image, which is electronically routed to cost center managers for online review and approval of the expenditure. This replaces a manual paper-intensive process whereby invoices were received in AP, copied, and then sent via internal mail for review and approval by the appropriate cost center manager.

- *eTimesheets.* Paper timesheets that were mailed or faxed to payroll twice a month have been replaced with a Web application. Employees record their hours electronically twice a month.
- *Travel planner.* Instead of calling a corporate travel office to coordinate reservations for business travel arrangements, most travel plans can be made by accessing an internal Web site and reserving airline tickets, hotel rooms, and rental cars.
- *Employee 401K and stock option statements viewable via an intranet.* Formerly, these were printed and mailed quarterly.
- *Ariba procurement.* Employees log in to the Web-based Ariba application to place orders through online catalogs. These orders are automatically routed to preferred vendors. This system replaces a paper-based system that required approvals and was mailed to Purchasing for creation of a PO and sourcing.
- *Financial reporting.* Managers with access to FIN!Web have real-time access to revenue and expense data for their assigned cost centers, and have the ability to electronically record accruals and reclasses. This replaces a system from which analysts ran endless reports each month for e-mail distribution to appropriate managers for review.

The last item shows just how much the game has changed. When the e-mail distribution methodology was introduced, it was considered a big improvement over the old system, from which reports were printed and distributed to the appropriate managers. And, indeed, it was a major improvement over the old; but, as this example demonstrates, just as quickly as something becomes a best practice, it becomes commonplace or standard and, eventually, obsolete.

Those who know Campos realize that she is not one to rest on her laurels or accomplishments. She has goals for the future—plans to take Schwab further down the information superhighway—and she shared some of those future enhancements. Specifically, she is looking at

- Web-based payments
- Electronic invoicing
- Electronic pay stubs
- eAction forms
- Web benefits enrollment

Clearly, Campos is a big fan of Web-based technologies. In closing her remarks at the conference, she noted, "There are countless opportunities for your company to improve both internal operating efficiency and the bottom line by putting the Web to work for you." Savvy AP professionals will follow her advice.

4

Master Vendor File

The master vendor file is one of the most overlooked aspects of the Accounting and Accounts Payable (AP) functions. Ignoring it can lead to trouble in the form of duplicate payments and increased risk for fraud. In this chapter, we look at

- Master vendor file setup
- Naming conventions
- Master vendor file changes
- Master vendor file cleanup

MASTER VENDOR FILE SETUP

Background

Setting up the master vendor file is one of those functions that no one really focuses on too much. However, handled ineffectually, it can and does lead to duplicate payments and opens the door to fraud. It contains the vital information about a company's vendors. The data contained in each master vendor file will vary from industry to industry. Usually, the responsibility for setting up vendors and maintaining them in the master vendor file resides in AP. Sometimes it is in Purchasing. Occasionally, each department has its own master vendor file, although this is generally not recommended.

Best Practices

Access to the master vendor file, for anything but information lookup, should be severely limited. Only a few people should be able to enter information, be it for setup or to make changes. Vendors should be set up on the master vendor file before any payments are made. Most companies will set up a vendor only if they believe there will be an ongoing relationship with that firm. One-time transactions are typically not set up in the master vendor file. Information in the files might include

- Vendor name (legal)
- DBA (the company's "doing business as" name)
- Business address
- Ship-To address
- Remit-To address
- Bill-To address (including a contact name)
- Phone number
- Fax number
- E-mail address
- Taxpayer identification number (TIN)/employer identification number (EIN)
- W-9 on file (Yes No)
- For electronic funds transfer (EFT) payments:
  - Name on bank account
  - Bank's routing number
  - Bank account number
  - Bank's automated clearinghouse (ACH) contact

- Bank's contact phone number
- Type of business (e.g., corporation, sole proprietorship, partnership—general or limited)

A form can be used to accumulate this data. Once the information has been compiled, authorized parities should approve (i.e., sign) it.

While most people believe the function belongs in AP, especially when many independent contractors are used, it is acceptable to have it in Purchasing, assuming all the rules are followed. Ideally, there should be only one master vendor file.

Each vendor should have one, and only one, master vendor file. When a vendor has several, the door is swung wide open for duplicate payments.

A strict naming convention should be adhered to when setting up master vendor files. While at first glance this may seem silly, there are very good reasons for it. For example, a company called The Red Door could be set up as any one of the following:

- The Red Door
- Red Door, The
- Red Door

There is no right or wrong way to set it up, just as long as the leading *The* is always treated in the same manner. Similarly, let's look at IBM to see what could go wrong. Here are a few ways the venerable computer company could be listed:

- IBM
- I B M
- I.B.M.
- International Business Machines

Without a naming convention, several files could be set up for the same company. This also makes it difficult for AP associates checking the master vendor file to ascertain if a payment has been made. Which IBM file should they look in?

Here are some guidelines you might use:

- For vendors commonly known by their initials or an acronym, use the initials or acronym rather than the full name (i.e., IBM, not International Business Machines).
- Do not use abbreviations, except when following the first guideline listed here (i.e., Olympia & York, not O&Y).
- Substitute the symbol "&" for "and" in vendor names (i.e., D&H, not D and H).
- Eliminate spaces and periods between initials (i.e., IBM, not I B M or I.B.M.).
- For individuals, list their first name, followed by a space, then their last name (i.e., Mary Schaeffer, not Schaeffer, Mary or Schaeffer Mary).
- Do not leave a space between Mc (or Mac) in either a company or an individual's name (i.e., MacDonald, not Mac Donald).

Companies typically assign a vendor number to each vendor. Companies also typically include in their vendor files their employees who travel. This is so T&E reimbursement payments can be made. Some use the employees' Social Security number as the employee ID number and in the master vendor file. With all the recent problems with identity theft, this once common practice should be eliminated. Employees who regularly receive payments should be assigned a vendor number that is different than the Social Security number. In fact, some question whether it is necessary to have this information for employees in the vendor file.

As it is often difficult to get W-9 information from independent contractors, making a completed W-9 form part of the process of setting up the master vendor file is a good idea. Without the completed form, the file cannot be set up and consequently the invoice cannot be processed for payment. Establishing the process in this manner takes the pressure off AP for being the bad guy refusing to make the payment.

Almost Best Practices

Few AP departments have the luxury of starting over with the master vendor file. Occasionally, when a new accounting system is put in, companies will take a thorough look at the master vendor file. However, it is never too late to start using best practices, and it is never too late to start with a naming convention. This won't help the old data but will get the master vendor file pointed in the right direction.

Reality Check for Accounts Payable

Although it is a best practice to get the W-9 before any checks are cut, a few management teams will not back this practice. Also, if the independent contractor is valued and/or needed, management may not stick to its guns in requiring the W-9.

Worst Practices

Worst practices include

- Allowing both AP and Purchasing to have their own master vendor file
- Allowing many people to set up vendors
- Having no naming convention

USING NAMING CONVENTIONS

Background

One of the reasons that duplicate payments occur is that there is sometimes more than one account set up in the master vendor file for the same company, as in the case of IBM discussed earlier. Readers probably have additional variations on the few mentioned. If stringent controls are not set around the master vendor file setup and/or the files are never purged, multiple entries for the same account will ensue. Consider the following very common scenario. The first time an account is set up, it is named IBM. The next time an invoice comes in, the AP associate looks for International Business Machines and, not finding the entry, sets up another account on the master vendor file using the longer name. Now a third invoice arrives and is paid under the IBM name, but it is paid late so IBM sends along another invoice marked "Second Notice." The AP associate checks under the longer name and, finding the invoice not paid in that account, goes ahead and pays it.

Hence, a duplicate payment is made. Some may think this is not a big deal and that IBM would likely return the duplicate payment. In the case of IBM, the duplicate payment probably would be returned—eventually. Researching unidentified cash is never a high priority for overworked suppliers, however, and the funds might not come back for a month. That's one month when the firm wouldn't have use of its money. And this is the best-case scenario.

In many cases suppliers don't return the funds, and that's why duplicate payment audit firms thrive. Suppliers frequently credit the customer's account for the duplicate payment and leave it there, never alerting the customer to the fact that the account has a credit balance.

Duplicate payments aren't the only potential problem. Multiple entries in the master vendor file open the door for unscrupulous employees to commit fraud.

Best Practices

There is one simple best practice when it comes to master vendor files: Use a standardized set of rules when naming accounts. This is sometimes referred to as *naming convention.* There is no right or wrong set of rules. The important thing is that there is a standard way to handle the issues that are likely to cause naming trouble: The rules are communicated to all affected parties and are adhered to. This communication should be to both the parties responsible for the account setup and everyone who must use the master vendor files for any reason.

Here is one set of rules that was developed by RECAP Inc.:

- If the name is a corporation that includes "Corp.," "Inc.," or "LLC," include that in the name when you set up the vendor.

- If the name of the vendor begins with an article (the, a, etc.), do not include it in the name when you set up the vendor.

- If the name is an individual, consistently include or exclude prefixes such as "Mr.," "Ms.," and "Dr."

- Avoid using periods with vendor names; use one space after each initial.

- Avoid abbreviations or be consistent in their use.

- Avoid using apostrophes in vendor names or in abbreviations of words in vendor names.

- Enter vendor names beginning with a number as specified; however, names that begin with a changing year, such as the "2004 U.S. Open Tennis," should be set up without the year prefix.

- If abbreviations are used, a short table of allowable abbreviations should be prepared and provided to people who are authorized to add vendors, as well as to people who have to find vendors based on a name. For example, "American" can be abbreviated either "Am" or "Amer." Decide on a standard and include it in the list.

- If the vendor is doing business as, trading as, or known as a name different from its actual name, use the actual name on the second line of the name or the first line of the address.
- If the vendor asks that you pay a factor, set up the name for the vendor and put the name of the factor as the second line of the name or the first line of the address.
- If the vendor is a taxing authority, set up the name of the taxing authority as the name. Put any qualifiers, such as department, division, and so on, on the second line of the name or the first line of the address. Despite instruction on many property tax bills that specify that you make a check out to the name of an individual as tax collector, the check will be cashed if you make it out to the name of the taxing authority as the first part of the vendor's name to indicate no data are missing.
- If your system does not support two-line names, consider using the first line of the address for the continuation of the vendor's name. If the vendor's name fits completely in the name field and the first line of the address is required, put a period in the first line of the address.

Almost Best Practices

There are no almost best practices here. You either use a standardized naming convention or not. Some companies have a few rules regarding naming, addressing issues like the article *The* and the use of titles and abbreviations. These are a good start in the right direction but still leave many loopholes open. For the naming convention to truly work it has to be thorough. Otherwise, the door will still be open a crack and the unscrupulous will find ways to smash right through.

Reality Check for Accounts Payable

Unless people are intimately aware of the issues relating to names like IBM and the problems they can cause, they will be incredulous when first presented with the standardized rules for naming accounts. Thus, once again, it will fall to the AP manager to educate the rest of the company as to why this is such an important issue.

Worst Practices

Worst practices include

- Ignoring the issue and having no set of standardized rules
- Not communicating the standards to all affected parties

MAKING CHANGES TO THE MASTER VENDOR FILE

Background

It would be nice if, once a supplier had been set up on the master vendor file, that was it. Unfortunately, at least as far as record maintenance is concerned, changes occasionally have to be made to the information. People leave, companies move, and phone numbers change. Additionally, if terms are included as part of the information in the master vendor file, they too change periodically. If proper care is not taken with who can make changes to the file and who can't, the company leaves itself wide open to fraud. Two simple changes to the Remit-To address could put a legitimate payment in the hands of a crook if a company is not careful. An unscrupulous employee with access to the master vendor file would simply change the Remit-To address for a supplier that is scheduled to receive a large check. After the check is cut and mailed, the employee then makes another change to the Remit-To address, returning it to the correct address. By the time the supplier complains, the check will have been cashed and it becomes exceedingly difficult to trace the problem. At that point, it would probably be assumed that the check was stolen out of the mail. Who would suspect that someone had tampered with the master vendor file? It might never even be considered.

Best Practices

Access to the master vendor file, for anything but information lookup, should be severely limited. Only a few people should be able to enter information, be it for setup or to make changes. A form should be used to standardize changes. Changes should also conform to the naming convention used when setting up the master vendor file in the first place. Those who have just read the best practices for setting up a master vendor file will note that there is a bit of overlap when it comes to making changes to the master vendor file. This makes sense. But do not stop there. There are additional best practices that should be employed when it comes to changes to the master vendor file.

A report should be generated weekly or monthly, depending on the number of changes made on average to the master vendor file. The report should detail all the changes made to the file in the given time period. It should include the names of the person requesting the change and the person authorizing the change. It might also include the date the last change was made. This report should be given directly to a senior-level executive and should be reviewed line by line for any odd-looking entries. The fact that this report is generated and reviewed should be common knowledge.

Companies that are very security conscious might want to run the report at different times during the year. In all cases, companies should have the ability to generate this report whenever needed.

Almost Best Practices

While it is desirable that a senior-level employee review changes made to the master vendor file, few senior executives will be willing to do this. It is more important that the report be reviewed on a very regular basis than having it go to a senior executive. In practice, companies might want to send it to two individuals for review—a senior executive and a middle manager.

Reality Check for Accounts Payable

It is unlikely that the senior executive will review the change report, except on a rare occasion—and that atypical event will be at the most inconvenient time. The middle manager assigned to review the report should do so and should mark it after each review. This could become an audit point, and this is not the place that any department wants to be written up on, especially if the company has experienced employee fraud.

Worst Practices

Worst practices include

- Having no formal process for inputting changes to the master vendor file
- Having no review process of the changes made to entries in the master vendor file
- Having no limits on who can make changes to the file

MASTER VENDOR FILE CLEANUP

Background

At many companies, once a vendor gets into its master vendor file it stays there forever. In a perfect world this would not be a problem. However, if an account is not used for a while and then the vendor becomes active, often a new master vendor file is set up. Then, and especially if no strict naming convention is used, there will be two or more master vendor files for the same vendor. This can lead to duplicate payments or worse. When a duplicate invoice arrives and one of the master vendor files is checked and no payment is found, a duplicate payment will be made against the second vendor file. Even worse, if an employee bent on fraud becomes aware of an inactive vendor file, the employee can use the inactive file as a cover for fraudulent practices.

Recent Institute of Management and Administration (IOMA) statistics show that close to 30 percent of companies never clean up their master vendor file, with smaller companies ignoring the task slightly more frequently than larger companies. More than 30 percent have a formal process that reviews and purges the master vendor file on an annual basis.

Best Practices

Once an account has been inactive for over a year, it should be purged from the company's master vendor files—or at least moved to inactive status. The activity should be maintained for several years. The policy and procedures for master vendor file cleanup should be incorporated into the AP and Purchasing formal written policy and procedures guidelines.

If the master vendor file has never been purged, hiring an outside firm that specializes in master vendor file cleanup might be appropriate. Not only will it get the job done if the rest of the staff is otherwise engaged, but it will also allow the company access to best practice methodology in use at other companies.

The experts say that master vendor file maintenance should be a process, not a project. Maintaining the master vendor file should be an *ongoing* process and not a one-shot project.

There are certain events that trigger a purge of the master vendor file when it hasn't been done in the past. They include, but are not limited to

- The installation of a new accounting package
- A merger
- An acquisition
- The hiring of a new controller or chief financial officer (CFO)

Take advantage of these events to bring up the issue of master vendor file maintenance and introduce best practices in this area.

Almost Best Practices

If the issue is not going to be addressed on an ongoing basis, the once-a-year review is probably an acceptable alternative.

Reality Check for Accounts Payable

If the master vendor file has never been purged and a new accounting system is being put in place, many companies choose to start over from scratch rather than try and purge the existing file. While this is a lot of work, it is sometimes easier than trying to sort through the mess that currently exists. It is not unusual to hear reports from companies that go through their master vendor file for the first time that indicate the company kept only 30 percent of the vendors in their old master vendor file.

Worst Practices

Worst practices include

- Never purging the master vendor file
- Haphazardly purging the master vendor file
- Having no one with direct authority or responsibility for the maintenance of the master vendor file

CASE STUDY

Experienced Accounts Payable Pro
Shares Master Vendor File
Control Secrets

After running an analysis of its master vendor file, AMF Bowling Worldwide Inc. discovered that some of its vendors were duplicated as many as 20 times. Thus, it is not surprising that it had 1.8 million vendor entries in the master vendor file. Michael W. Baynes, the company's process systems resolution administrator, had his work cut out for him.

THE SOLUTION

The most important step is to get control of the input before you even attempt to clean up anything, warns Baynes. He recommends restricting access to vendor setup to a limited group of trained people who understand "naming conventions," the U.S. Postal Service rules of addressing, and the IRS preferred reporting criteria. Once that was done, he was ready to get started. Initially, he suggests taking the following steps:

1. Identify exactly the purpose of the cleanup.
2. Identify research and cleanup priorities.
3. Make the members of the Information Systems (IS) department your friends—you will need them.
4. Decide if you have the resources to handle cleanup within AP. If not, consider consultants who may be contracted.
5. Make sure AP controls this process and makes all the calls from beginning to end. If not, the audit trail vanishes.

It was then time to address the tough parts. The 1.8 million entries in the master vendor file were not manageable. Baynes suggests determining a cutoff point for active vendors that is comfortable, based on the last time you paid a vendor and the likelihood of doing business with it again. He then split off inactive vendors to a file of their own. This data was not deleted but rather was made accessible only to the vendor setup staff, for emergency reference. He did this with help from the IS staff.

The remaining data can then be put into the database or spreadsheet program with which you are most comfortable. Baynes chose Excel. He sorted it by company name first to eliminate the obvious duplicate vendors. Then try other kinds of sorting. For example, you might sort by TIN, phone number, or address. Review the file after each of these sorts to identify additional obvious duplicates.

Once the criteria for inclusion in the master vendor file were established, Baynes reviewed it each week for vendors to be deleted. These are included in a report to management. He also insists on W-9s from vendors before paying them the first time to ensure no year-end 1099 problems.

From 2001 to the present, the company has been able to reduce processing expenses by approximately 34 percent due to improvements in accessing and using the master vendor file.

ATTACK THE MASTER VENDOR FILE YOURSELF

Here are the steps that Baynes uses to eliminate obvious duplicates:

1. Dump your master file into a manageable database. Excel is preferred.
2. Be sure your file contains all of the following:
   - Vendor number
   - Vendor name
   - Address
   - TIN
   - 1099 reporting classification
   - Personal/Corp Code (PCN). This is different in some systems. In JD Edwards, for example, this tells us whether it is a sole proprietor, corporation, or noncorporate entity such as a partnership, medical vendor, or attorney.
3. Sort the file by name first to locate obvious duplications. Remedy this by moving duplicates to your inactive vendor file, making sure the ones you keep active satisfy all reporting criteria. Don't make work for yourself by shortcutting this step. The rules we mentioned in the very first paragraph must be adhered to.
4. While you are addressing duplications, it is a good time to address the naming conventions, which include eliminating the word *the* and the use of "county of," "state of," "town of," and so forth. Also, don't abbreviate the object name of a vendor. VA Trucking Co. will not be in the same alphabetical place as Virginia Trucking Co., even though it is the same vendor.

5. Initiate and develop a method of reporting these changes so users will be aware. Sales and product groups are critical users and need be kept in the loop.

6. Try various sorts. You may want to sort by TIN to find duplications, but be aware that duplications here may just be a subsidiary or branch. For example, a vendor may have over 500 locations nationally but just one TIN.

7. Since each of these vendors needs to have proper reporting information, you may need to sort the file to show where you are missing tax numbers, 1099 classification codes, and so on. Sorting by each field, you will find the holes in your 1099 reporting that can be corrected to prevent errors in reporting to the IRS.

8. Locate the person at your company who handles the B notices that the IRS sends out annually in August. This will show the areas that need to be addressed and were not in the past. If this process is not in AP, consideration should be given to moving it there. Vendor setup reflects on this process more than any other. This will probably help negate fines and levies from the IRS.

MANAGEMENT REPORTS

Let's face it—after all that work, you should definitely produce several reports to both validate the work and inform management of what's been done. Baynes points out that these reports may start off as a function of your IS department, but they can be set up to run on demand in AP—no matter what your IS department tells you. Here are the reports he suggests:

- *Inactive vendor (IV) report.* This report is a weekly listing of vendors moved from the master vendor file.

- *Open amounts report.* This is a weekly report accessing the IV file for open invoices, purchase orders (POs), credits, and others that will require correction or completion of previous activity. The IV file will notoriously have open items come about because of constant additions. This is normal and will actually improve your audit status.

- *New vendor additions report.* This monthly report should be a concise listing of *all* vendors added or changed in the master vendor file. We strongly recommend that this be reviewed by a senior-level executive and that it be widely known that it is being reviewed. This is a deterrent against internal fraud.

Baynes notes that you may add the IV file as an option and separate report too.

In this way, you may have a date-to-date listing also during a defined period (e.g., 07/01/03 to 08/01/03). This may be dumped into Excel, and each vendor may be audited for correct entry status. This is the report that keeps your ongoing processes clean. It should be reviewed and corrections noted and processed.

The AP manager needs to verify that corrections were made to the master vendor file. This report should be flexible enough to be run over any time frame you wish. Baynes has run it for periods as short as one day and as long as two years. This is *not* a dollar-activity report. If you use dollar-activity criteria in this report, a large number of your entries will not show.

Two reports that can be run when setting up a new vendor will help identify potential duplicate vendors:

- *Name search query.* This system report allows you to initiate a search of your files (both master and IV if you wish) for a vendor name or partial key word, which results in a listing of all vendors that have that key word in their name. This will aid in preventing duplications.

- *Taxpayer ID query.* This system report allows functions identical to the name search query except the TIN is used as the search object.

5

P-Cards

P-cards, also called corporate procurement cards or purchasing cards, have hit the corporate landscape in a big way in the last few years. Similar in many respects to the credit cards many people carry, these corporate payment vehicles have some very real differences that need to be addressed. In this chapter, we investigate the

- Design of the p-card program
- Establishing procedures
- Setting controls
- Increasing usage
- 1099s and p-cards
- Terms
- Rebates

DESIGN OF THE P-CARD PROGRAM

Background

While most people understand what a p-card is, not everyone realizes that the p-card program needs to be well thought out and the mechanics of how it will work spelled out to employees.

Best Practices

Each company should have a formal policy with regard to its p-card program. The National Association of Purchasing Card Professionals (NAPCP) suggests that the following elements be spelled out in the p-card policy given to all affected employees, including the administrative assistants of those executives who use p-cards:

- The business case in order for employees to gain an understanding of the importance of using the process
- A definition of targeted transactions as well as those that are excluded
- Transaction and monthly spending limits
- User procedures, including initial card activation, receipt and record retention, and time frame expectations
- Preferred suppliers
- Procedures related to lost/stolen accounts
- An explanation of decline potential and appropriate procedures
- Cardholder agreement of responsibility

The policy should be updated periodically, ideally whenever a change is made or, at a minimum, once every year. These changes should be reflected in the policy and communicated to all affected employees.

The policy can be published on the Internet or intranet site for easy access by all employees.

New employees should be given the policy as well as an overview as part of their welcome packet.

Almost Best Practices

Review the policy for possible updates every two years. Publish updates only if there are changes. Letting the policy go longer than two years without a review can cause problems and can also cause the company to miss out on potential new features or cost-saving initiatives.

Reality Check for Accounts Payable

Reviewing the p-card policy is one of those chores that is likely to get lost in the shuffle. Make it part of the annual review or a summer task or some other function. Doing so will ensure that the policy is looked at periodically to see how well it continues to fit the company and whether there are improvements that could be made.

Worst Practices

Worst practices include letting the policy sit on the shelf gathering dust, never to be looked at again. Companies that do this also tend to let the p-card program wither, with no one taking ownership and making it thrive. This is a potential opportunity for an Accounts Payable (AP) manager looking to enhance his or her reputation within the firm.

ESTABLISHING PROCEDURES

Background

In order for a p-card program to work effectively, procedures for all affected parties must be established. Without a formalized plan of how the program will work, a program can flounder and duplicate payments will occur. Also, the firm will not maximize the usage or cost-saving possible. Remember, for the most part, one of the main reasons that companies use p-cards is to reduce the number of small-dollar invoices in AP.

Best Practices

Begin by providing the policy and procedure guide as previously described to all employees. Also, spell out in clear detail

- The process for using the card
- The process and timing for the reconciliation of all cardholder statements
- What should be done with the receipts received from the vendors
- What can and cannot be purchased on the card. For example, some companies do not allow the purchase of inventory materials, and others do not allow the use with 1099 vendors. There is no right or wrong answer on using a p-card with these items, just the need for a policy.
- The approval process, if there is one

The penalties for noncompliance should be spelled out clearly.

Input on the process should be obtained from all affected parties. This will make it more likely that they will comply with the rules and use the card as much as possible.

Ideally, the procedures should be posted on the AP Internet page or the company intranet.

Procedures should be reviewed annually to ensure that they mirror what is currently being done in the company. When the program is first getting off the ground, the procedures should be updated every six months.

Almost Best Practices

Almost best practices include issuing formal policy and procedures without getting input. This can lead to some resistance if AP has created work for other departments instead of simplifying their lives.

Reality Check for Accounts Payable

Expect some resistance to the p-card program when it is first rolled out. However, if you take the time to educate managers and employees who are reluctant to use the card, the program will eventually prosper. Sometimes the biggest complainers turn into the most vocal advocates when they see the advantages of the program.

Worst Practices

Worst practices include allowing certain vendors to submit invoices for certain purchases and accept p-cards for others. This leads to great confusion in the AP department and duplicate payments. Some vendors honestly can't suppress the printing of invoices, while others don't put too much effort into the process.

SETTING CONTROLS

Background

One of the most frequent objections to p-card use is the concern that the cards will not be used properly and put the company at risk. In actuality, there has been little reported improper card use, and the risk objection can be easily overcome by ensuring that the proper controls are in place.

Best Practices

When it comes to controls, companies have numerous areas where they can rein in use of cards or limit it as they see fit. Here are a few things they can do:

- *Empower all trusted employees needing a card.* By giving the card to only trusted employees, employers can give themselves some level of comfort. Many have great success by having employees who are authorized to use the card sign a statement saying that the employee understands that any misuse of the card will result in automatic termination. This can serve as a powerful deterrent.

- *Set card guidelines and procedures.* When a procurement card program is begun, detailed guidelines and procedures should be established. Copies of these regulations should be distributed to all affected employees. While this seems obvious, it is not always done.

- *Limit the dollar amount of each transaction.* This is certainly a good way to minimize losses should fraud occur. The dollar limit can vary by employee and is usually related not only to the level of trust but the actual need the employee might be expected to have. These limits can always be changed if it is determined that the original level was not high enough.

- *Limit the dollar amount that can be spent each month by each employee.* In addition to the dollar amount each employee can spend per transaction, it is also possible to give each a monthly allowance. This, too, can vary by employee and area of responsibility. This control device limits the amount of risk a company has with the card. Most who use the card establish per-charge and monthly limits.

- *Use Standard Industrial Classification (SIC) code blockouts.* Companies concerned that an employee will take the card and go Christmas shopping or take a trip to Tahiti can use SIC blockouts. By disallowing charges at certain SIC codes, a company mitigates this issue. Of course, this matter can be resolved by the dollar limits placed on the employee for each transaction and for each month. If an employee would charge a vacation on a

company credit card, the company has other, bigger issues with this person.

- *Set a departmental budget.* Another fear associated with
  corporate procurement cards is that everyone will go
  out and charge crazily, buying things for the office that
  are *not* absolutely necessary. This, of course, rarely happens, but by setting budget levels at the departmental
  level, management has control over the big picture.

- *Insist on a monthly review of all charge card statements and
  have a supervisor's signature on each statement.* This after-
  the-fact review will uncover any spending that might be
  slightly off base. It also assures management that the
  proper oversight is being given to all expenditures, and
  improper spending not otherwise detected might turn
  up. In one of the rare cases in which a card was abused,
  an employee was buying a computer for himself—piece
  by piece. One month a hard drive was purchased, the
  next a printer, then the central processing unit (CPU),
  and so on. Without the supervisory review, these items
  might have slipped through since they fell within the
  dollar amount and SIC codes allowed.

- *Reserve the right to review.* At any point in time, senior
  management should be able to come in and review the
  statements for the entire company or any one department or individual. It is not a bad idea to have internal
  auditors, and perhaps even the external auditors, periodically spot-check the statements.

- *Set up workable dispute resolution procedures with vendors.* One
  of the advantages of receiving an invoice that doesn't
  need to be paid for 30 or more days is the leverage it
  gives to the purchaser. If the goods turn out to be sub-
  standard or defective in any way, the purchaser can with-
  hold all or part of the payment. This can then force the
  supplier to negotiate in good faith. If the supplier has

been paid, it has less incentive to resolve disputes. In fact, the only incentive it has is the promise of future business. By establishing dispute procedures in advance, the purchaser avoids this issue. Some might think that the vendor may have little interest in developing such a mechanism, but remember two things: First, the vendor wants to do additional business and thus needs to placate its customers. Second, the vendor is also interested in using the p-card. It lowers costs on both sides of the table. If a customer is dissatisfied with the service received when the p-card is used, it will stop using it—forcing the vendor back to more costly billing and collection procedures.

- *Set supplier guidelines.* This will guard against the card's being used inappropriately. It will also put the vendors on notice as to what is expected. Remember, in most cases both the buyer and the seller benefit from the use of the p-card.

- *Institute card cancellation procedures.* This puts everyone on notice that the card can be revoked at any time the corporation sees fit. This is especially important in the instance of employee termination. Regardless of the reason, the AP manager will want the ability to immediately cancel the card. This should be done even if the parting is amicable or the employee has left of his own volition. Not canceling a card under these circumstances is begging for trouble. Most card issuers will be able to handle this requirement.

Almost Best Practices

At a minimum, individual employees should have controls set regarding the dollar amounts they can charge and the types of items they can purchase. This information needs to be communicated to the employees so there is no misunderstanding.

Reality Check for Accounts Payable

No matter how hard AP works to establish controls over the program, there will always be exceptions that don't fit into the big picture. Whenever those loopholes appear, work to adjust the procedures so the controls prevent misuse or inappropriate use.

Worst Practices

Worst practices include having no controls built into the program, allowing employees to use the card as they see fit. Sometimes companies, in a zest to expand their programs, forget about controls. The end result is duplicate payments.

INCREASING USAGE

Background

Companies love p-cards because they get small-dollar invoices out of the AP process, ultimately making the AP department more efficient. Growth in the p-card arena is sometimes limited due to constraints that can be addressed.

Best Practices

Ways to increase p-card usage include

- Educating everyone who has a card about all the potential opportunities to use the p-card
- Expanding the number of merchants in the p-card program
- Expanding the dollar limits of those authorized to use p-cards
- Looking for new opportunities to use the card. This can include things like paying for subscriptions, office supplies, and so on.

- Offering cards to employees who make frequent small-dollar purchases
- Whenever an invoice comes in that could have been paid for with a p-card, sending it back to the approver suggesting it be paid for with the p-card

Almost Best Practices

Refuse to pay any invoice for which a p-card could be used.

Reality Check for Accounts Payable

Before refusing to pay any invoice for which a p-card could be used, make sure you have management backing. Otherwise, AP could end up with egg on its face.

Worst Practices

Worst practices include not encouraging the use of p-cards at every opportunity, especially when the company has gone through the trouble and expense of setting up a program.

1099s AND P-CARDS

Background

The use of p-cards presents a problem when they are used to pay independent contractors. In these situations, a 1099 must be issued. The problem is, of course, that the company using the p-card

- Often doesn't realize that there is a 1099 issue
- May not realize the vendor should get a 1099
- May realize that the vendor should get a 1099 but has no way of obtaining the necessary taxpayer identification number (TIN) information

Best Practices

The NAPCP recommends several practices that help get 1099s issued wherever required, including

- *Systems reporting.* Most p-card programs are managed through the use of internally or externally developed reporting systems. A common functionality within these systems is the flagging of 1099-MISC suppliers. The information provided by these systems will have to be combined with other payment systems and 1099-MISCs filed. One of the challenges to be addressed using this approach is determining who notifies whom that a supplier requires the 1099-MISC flag be turned on. The advantage of this approach is that you are not carte blanche excluding 1099-MISC suppliers who otherwise are a good fit for the program. The disadvantage is that you must manage the communication of 1099-MISC suppliers from cardholder to program administrator.
- *Specific 1099-MISC card.* Some end-user organizations issue a specific card that is used only for 1099-MISC supplier(s) or purposes so that the total on that/those cards is isolated. 1099-MISC reporting would be required on these purchases. The advantage of this approach is that 1099 spending is isolated. The disadvantage is the coordination required on the part of the requisitioner and cardholder.

Almost Best Practices

One method that generally works for identifying a corporation (which can be eliminated for 1099 purposes) is by looking for "Corp.," "Inc.," or "P.C." in its name. However, this approach is not foolproof as some suppliers use this nomenclature falsely.

Some companies simply exclude 1099 vendors from their p-card programs. Excluding 1099-MISC suppliers can be done to varying degrees, ranging from totally excluding these suppliers to excluding them in general policy and then following up through the use of data mining for noncompliance. The advantage of excluding 1099-MISC suppliers is the reduction of the risk of noncompliance with 1099-MISC requirements. The disadvantage of this approach is limiting the use of the p-card and the resulting benefits.

Reality Check for Accounts Payable

All issuers have the ability to provide 1099 data. Depending on the network used (American Express, MasterCard, or Visa), 1099 and TIN data are provided in a variety of ways. In addition to gaining an understanding as to how the networks provide information, another factor influencing 1099 and TIN data delivery is the data delivery process used by the card issuer. As part of the request for proposal (RFP) process or during the implementation phase, you need to gain an understanding as to how this data is delivered. In addition to relying on data provided by the card issuer, you will want to consider applying the approaches listed here.

Worst Practices

Worst practices include completely ignoring the 1099 issue when it comes to payments made with p-cards.

TERMS

Background

How the corporate p-card bill is paid can affect a company's bottom line. Just as companies routinely negotiate payment terms with other suppliers, they should also handle their p-card obligations similarly. After all, if the program is effective, the bill is likely to be one of a company's larger obligations.

Best Practices

The NAPCP advises companies to negotiate favorable terms for the payment of the p-card bill. In most instances, payment on these cards is expected within 7 days of receipt of the bill. A number of companies have succeeded in getting these terms extended to 14 and even 21 days. A company with an average bill of $1 million each month might be able to add $25,000 to its bottom line by getting the card issuer to agree to accept payment on day 21 instead of day 7, assuming it invested the money at 5 percent. Those borrowing at higher rates would have an even greater savings. While this might not seem like an extravagant amount of money to many, it's not a bad return for the few conversations it might take to get the card issuer to agree to these terms. Those just setting up a program might make the payment terms one of the negotiating points, especially if several issuers are bidding for the business.

Almost Best Practices

Almost best practices include paying at the terms offered by the card issuer.

Reality Check for Accounts Payable

If the program is not large enough, the issuer may be reluctant to negotiate payment terms. If that happens, revisit the issue when the program expands to several hundred thousand dollars per month. At lower levels it is unlikely that the issuer will be receptive to your overtures.

Worst Practices

Worst practices include paying the bill before the due date, effectively giving the supplier an added advantage.

REBATES

Background

Companies that spend a significant amount of money on their p-cards have found that card issuers will compete for their business. In fact, to get the business, some will even offer rebates based on the level of purchases.

Best Practices

Negotiate rebates from the card issuer. This is a subject the card issuer will never initiate, warns the NAPCP. However, conversations with numerous managers reveal that this is going on at certain levels. In order to qualify for these rebates, your company will need to make purchases using the card at a reasonably high level.

It has been suggested that the minimum program should be about $500,000 per month in expenditures on the card before the issuer will even entertain discussions about a rebate. Rebates are generally quoted in basis points, with 100 basis points equaling 1 percent. At this level, a company might expect a rebate in the neighborhood of 5 basis points or $25,000 per month, or $300,000 on an annual basis. As programs get larger, the number of basis points the card issuer is willing to rebate grows. It has also been suggested that really big programs might be able to earn as many as 50 basis points in rebates. As with the terms, this issue can be used as a negotiating point when establishing a new program with several issuers bidding for the business.

Almost Best Practices

Ask for rebates, but don't necessarily take the first offer. If the card issuer believes the business may go elsewhere, it may become more aggressive in its offer. At a minimum, ask at least once—even if you feel your volume doesn't justify a rebate now. Let the card issuer know what you are thinking and plant the seed so that down the road, when volume increases, the issuer is ready to give your company the rebate.

Reality Check for Accounts Payable

This is definitely a case of "Those who don't ask don't get." In order for the company to get a rebate, it must request one—ideally during the negotiation process when the account is being set up. If you have a program in place without a rebate feature and the business is significant, try bringing up the topic. If the card issuer is not receptive, you might suggest (with senior management's backing) that you are considering putting the program out for bid.

Worst Practices

Worst practices include never asking for rebates.

CASE STUDY

P-Cards Improve Accounts Payable Process at PETsMART, Rock-Tenn, and Rouse

Initially designed to rid corporate America's AP departments of the burgeoning number of small-dollar invoices, p-cards are now being used by innovative companies for a lot more. Speaking at a recent conference, three savvy professionals revealed the strategies being used at their companies to streamline operations through expanded use of p-cards. The program, moderated by the National Association of Purchasing Card Professionals' Laura Flandrick, brought together professionals from three very different companies who shared their success strategies as well as their plans for the future of p-cards at their organizations.

OVERVIEW

Flandrick began the session by sharing some illuminating statistics about the use of p-cards by Corporate America. She strongly believes that there will be significant growth in coming years in the use of p-cards. Various statistics show that current market usage is only about 20 percent of what it could be. The trend is toward an increasing average transaction size, growing from approximately $200 in 1998 to somewhere between $240 and $250 in 2000.

Other p-card metrics show that between 1998 and 2000

- Monthly spending increased 29 percent.
- Monthly spending per card increased 36 percent.
- Monthly increases in the number of transactions per card grew 23 percent.
- Cardholders as a percentage of employees increased 75 percent.
- Purchases made on the p-card increased 54 percent.

Flandrick also pointed out that organizations with p-card programs view them as positive and that p-cards are becoming an accepted method of doing business at midmarket companies. Alternative payment methods do not seem likely to replace them. Finally, she reported that the fears that some companies had about loss of control with p-cards appear to be subsiding. Given all these facts, Flandrick believes that p-cards are here to stay and are likely to take a bigger piece of the payment pie in upcoming years.

P-CARDS AT PETsMART

Assistant Treasurer Brad Larson had no intention of using p-cards until his company hired a new chief financial officer (CFO) who was a strong proponent of the cards. When his new boss asked him to look into p-cards, Larson explained to him that he had tried them about five years ago and he did not believe they would work in a retail environment.

Fortunately, no matter how much Larson explained, his boss was determined. His "I don't think you understand" was met with "I think you ought to look at p-cards to get rid of petty cash." Larson didn't get to his position as director of treasury/assistant treasurer by refusing to follow his boss's suggestions. So he set about investigating a p-card program to be used to eliminate petty cash, but he had a hidden agenda. He says he is stubborn and opinionated and was determined to demonstrate that p-cards would not work in a retail environment. He came away from the exercise wondering why he hadn't come up with the idea on his own many years before. The program was so successful in getting rid of petty cash that the company is now looking at a one-card program. He also says he wishes he had started with procurement instead of petty cash.

For Larson, the p-card program helped identify other areas where attention was needed. The company discovered that it needed policies for money it didn't even know was being spent. The individual stores' use of petty cash concealed certain spending categories. One of these concealed categories revealed by p-card data was the amount being spent at florists. At first glance, something seemed out of place. Why were pet stores buying flowers? After some investigation, it was discovered that individual stores would buy employees flowers to celebrate a birth, a graduation, or other similar event. The company then devised a policy to cover such purchases. Larson noted that $30 arrangements convey the same congratulatory message as $150 arrangements.

Similarly, the company was able to aggregate data and identify potential rebate opportunities. When it discovered that $50,000 had been spent at Pizza Hut, it realized that a price reduction could be arranged. However, when these amounts were paid out of the petty cash box, there was no audit trail and no way of capturing the information.

Although Larson believes that they have just scratched the surface of the potential savings, two days of work per month have been saved from AP. Seventy percent of petty cash payouts have also been eliminated. Users of the card no longer have to complete expense reimbursement forms and wait for settlement.

He worked with Internal Audit and Loss Prevention when setting up the program to ensure that proper controls were put in place. The controls, the price negotiations, and time savings are the three items he identifies as strengths of the program. On the other side of the coin, like many others, he counts the 1099 reporting as a weakness of the program. However, he contends that, with the petty cash program, the company had no 1099 reporting, so even poor reporting is an improvement.

He points out another benefit to the program. His department has gotten some good exposure with management and other departments. In closing, he listed the following savings to the company in addition to the rebates:

- AP processing time
- Reduced fraud losses
- Price negotiations
- New policies and procedures

ROCK-TENN COMPANY'S P-CARD PROGRAM

Cathy Sumeracki did not approach the p-card project at her company with the same skepticism as Larson had. The company had high hopes for the program. This paperboard manufacturer wanted to eliminate its low-dollar, indirect-spend invoices under $1,000. It estimates that this would be 22 percent of indirect-spend invoices and 11 percent of all invoices. Sumeracki knows the program is succeeding. In addition to the metrics that show the spending per month, she also has noticed

- Reduction in the number of vendors added as the use of the p-card grew
- A big reduction in the number of copies (of invoices) required
- Like PETsMART, a reduction in petty cash

A side benefit to the program is the fact that people in the field actually like the program, a welcome relief from the way most home-office initiatives are received. She is working with accounting to reap the full benefits of the program. She notes that the comprehensive controls are both a strength and a weakness. The difficulty is that the program emulated the current accounting practices at the company, which may be overkill given the size of most of the p-card purchases. It is an example of the old "spending a dollar to audit a dime" pattern.

P-CARDS AT THE ROUSE COMPANY

The Rouse Company is reconfiguring its accounts payable world, says Susan Wagner, the company's manager of Corporate Purchasing and AP. One of the ways the company was able to free personnel to work in the new functions was through the introduction of a p-card program. The reduction in the number of invoices freed up the time of a number of AP bookkeepers for other functions.

The company initially targeted low-dollar invoices. In its second year of operation, it took a closer look at the vendors providing services to the company. It aggressively pushed the program, asking vendors and contractors if they accepted p-cards. If the answer was affirmative, the company immediately began paying that way. Wagner says that only a few tried to renegotiate their contracts. This is because they realized they were getting their money faster and did not want to jeopardize the payment timing. The company no longer limits p-cards to small-dollar purchases.

Like others, Rouse was able to take a look at its spending and reduce the number of vendors by taking advantage of those who accepted p-cards. It created more national and regional contracts. The only weakness Wagner sees in the program is that the program administrators are not available 24/7. As the operator of many shopping centers, Rouse has employees using the cards seven days a week. If there is a problem on weekends or during off-hours, there is no one available to help them. She is looking into ways to address this problem.

CONCLUDING THOUGHTS

P-cards are one of the tools being used at companies in all different industries to streamline the payment process. Those whose companies are reluctant to try them might follow the PETsMART route of using them to eliminate petty cash. Auditors who are reluctant to approve a p-card program often see the light when they realize it could mean getting rid of the petty-cash function.

Accounts payable professionals who can find ways to use this innovative tool will not only help modernize the payment process and improve departmental productivity, they will also improve their image with management. Those who are interested in learning about the latest innovations in the p-card world should consider attending one of NAPCP's annual conferences. For details go to *www.napcp.org*.

6

Travel and Entertainment

Travel and entertainment (T&E) expenditures are the second largest controllable expense for most corporations. It is an area that causes a great amount of controversy. In this chapter, we take a look at

- Formal policy
- Cash advances
- T&E report form
- Verifying data
- Handling receipts
- Reservations
- Reimbursing employees
- Unused tickets

FORMAL POLICY

Background

The T&E policy should spell out the guidelines for company employees when it comes to travel and entertainment. It details some or all of the following:

119

- What is allowable
- What is not allowable
- How documentation should be submitted
- What approvals are necessary
- Timing of reporting
- If cash advances are permitted and, if so, under what circumstances
- If corporate T&E cards must be used
- Reimbursement policy
- What hotel chains are preferred or required
- What airlines are preferred or required
- What car rental agencies are recommended or required
- Whether employees must stay over on a Saturday night if a lower fare can be obtained
- How unused tickets are to be handled

Best Practices

The company's T&E policy should be formal, written, and distributed to all employees for easy reference. It should be updated periodically, no less frequently than once every two years. Ideally, the update should take place every year. Changes should be reflected in the policy, which is often printed and distributed in a binder.

Printing costs can be reduced almost entirely by publishing the T&E policy on the corporate intranet site. In this way, updates can be communicated quickly.

Whenever there is a major change to the T&E policy, a memo should go out from a senior executive explaining the change. The memo, which can be paper based or sent in an e-mail, should be sent to all employees.

For a T&E policy to be effective, it has to be enforced across the board. This means that managers should not be allowed to override the policy, where they think it does not apply to their staff. Obviously, for the policy to be effective it also needs to be adhered to by executives at all levels.

Policy enforcement should not fall on the shoulders of the Accounts Payable (AP) department. That really is not fair. Companies using an automated system can have a policy compliance feature built in. In these systems, reports that are in violation of the company policy are flagged for further investigation. The AP department can then return these reports to the approver's supervisor for further review.

Some of the more advanced automated systems take policy compliance one step further. They refuse to allow the submission of reports in violation of the policy. This is a bit extreme, as there will infrequently be occasions when an expense outside the policy is justified.

New employees should be given a copy of the T&E policy as part of their welcome packet.

Ideally, there should be a focal point for questions relating to the T&E policy.

Frequent T&E policy violators should be noted and their reports checked thoroughly each time one is submitted. (See the "Verifying Data" section later in this chapter.)

Senior management must support the policy in a very public way. Some companies do this effectively by having either the chief executive officer (CEO) or the chief financial officer (CFO) sign the cover memo that goes out with the policy. Others do it by having one of these senior officials sign a memo about T&E policy compliance that is put in the front of the T&E policy manual.

Almost Best Practices

Some companies, as well as employees with limited office space, think that giving each employee his or her own copy of the T&E manual is cost prohibitive. This might be true in the case of employees who travel only once or twice a year. These companies might have one manual per department stored in the common area. The problem with this approach is that, inevitably, one employee takes the manual into his or her office and forgets to return it. Then, when someone else needs it, the manual is not available.

The advent of inexpensive Internet and intranet sites has made the T&E manual issue less critical. Posting the policy on the Web turns this almost best practice into a best practice. Some companies simply post the manual on their Web site, not really caring who looks at it. This alleviates the need for passwords and so on. The truth be told, rarely are there any corporate secrets in the T&E policy. Thus, for most companies, posting the policy on the Web poses little or no risk.

Reality Check for Accounts Payable

No matter how good you are about educating employees about the T&E policy, via e-mail updates, memos, copies of the manual, and the Internet, calls will still come into AP about the policy. Additionally, violations will continue to appear on T&E reimbursement requests. A few flagrant violators will continue to claim "Nobody told me that," regardless of the vigilant efforts of the AP education team. The goal should be to wear these people down, forcing compliance through whatever means the company's policy allows. This can sometimes mean refusing to pay for flagrant policy violations—but only with very senior management–level support!

Worst Practices

Worst practices include

- Uneven enforcement of the policy, which can lead to additional violations and higher costs

- No policy
- An outdated policy
- An unclear policy

CASH ADVANCES

Background

Before corporate credit cards were commonplace, employees would routinely pay for all their travel expenses themselves. Airline tickets had to be booked and paid for weeks, if not months, in advance. Upon completion of a trip, they would submit their T&E expense form to obtain their reimbursement, as they do today. The difference was that traveling employees could be out of pocket for significant amounts of money, especially if they traveled frequently, to foreign countries, or first class.

Thus, the practice of cash advances evolved. To help the financially overburdened traveling executive, companies would advance them some amount of cash to cover these expenses. Upon the completion of the trip(s) and the expense report, the two would be reconciled and a settling up would occur. More often than not, this entailed the employee's writing a check for the amount he or she owed the company. If you are sitting there scratching your head, consider the following facts:

- There usually were no limits on the cash advance.
- There was no interest charged on the cash advance loan.
- Interest rates for the last 30 years were high (or very high) compared with today's rates.
- Few employees are willing to pay out of pocket when their employers offer a no-cost alternative—the cash advance.

This is not to say that all employees abused the cash advance system. Nothing could be farther from the truth. Not only did some abuse it, but the fact that employees were not paying out of pocket removed the biggest incentive to getting them to file their reimbursement forms.

The other factor affecting cash advances is that, in a very few cases, employees are tempted to fabricate expenses to justify not returning the cash.

Finally, there are the financial implications and procedural inefficiencies of the cash advance process. In higher-interest-rate environments, the lost interest income or the increased borrowing costs associated with cash advances were a factor. Even today, in a relatively low-interest-rate situation, there are cash flow implications. When cash advances are used, they have to be accounted for correctly and issued in the form of either cash or checks. Neither process adds value.

Best Practices

Don't issue cash advances. Let employees use their T&E cards to pay for most of their travel-related expenditures and pay for cash expenditures out of their own pocket. This will encourage timely submission of T&E expense reports after trips.

Almost Best Practices

Not every company is willing to take the "just say no to cash advances" stance. It may go against the corporate culture, or it may not be feasible given the level of employees who are asked to travel on the company's behalf. If advances are given, they should be only under special circumstances, with the approval of both the individual's direct supervisor and the supervisor's supervisor. Make it difficult, not impossible, so people will consider seriously before asking for an advance.

If a cash advance is provided, do it in the form of a check or an electronic (automated clearinghouse [ACH]) credit. Giving cash advances in the form of cash is rife with procedural issues and can lead to abuses.

Reality Check for Accounts Payable

It is unlikely that cash advances will completely go away. The goal is simply to minimize the times when they must be given. Work with those requesting cash advances to find other alternatives.

Worst Practices

Worst practices include

- Routinely giving cash advances
- Not following up with employees who receive cash advances to make sure expense reports are submitted on a timely basis
- Using cash for cash advances
- Not using a consistent policy for cash advances

T&E REPORT FORM

Background

The variety of forms provided by companies to their employees for the submission of their T&E expenses is vast. It ranges from the online sophisticated approach to the hand-drawn form that has been copied so many times it is full of speckles. Most companies fall somewhere in between, although you'd be surprised how many fall toward the lower end of the spectrum.

Falling in between, and probably more commonplace, are

the home-grown automated forms, typically developed on an Excel spreadsheet. The beauty of these forms is that formulas can be embedded in the worksheets so the employee does not have to do the math. This eliminates the mathematical errors. The formulas can be locked, preventing the employee from tampering with the evidence. Some of these in-house–developed forms are advanced and work perfectly fine for even rather large midsize companies.

Best Practices

Any automated form, whether it be created on a system purchased from a third party or developed in-house, can be e-mailed first for approvals and then to AP for submission. This makes the process much smoother and provides tracking information for those who want to know the status of their expense reports, reimbursements, and travel card payments. As previously stated, the formulas should be locked.

If the form is automated, policy compliance can be incorporated in some of the more advanced systems. This is ideal, especially at a large company. It also takes the burden off the AP staff, who really should not have to monitor for policy compliance. By having the system flag policy violations, the company can take appropriate action with offending employees to bring them into compliance.

Reporting can also be done to aggregate where funds are being spent. This information can then be used to negotiate better rates with preferred suppliers.

It should be noted that when we talk about policy violations, we do not necessarily mean outrageous spending. A violation could be something as simple as not flying on the preferred carrier, not using the company travel agent, or not flying the cheapest route because it meant stopping over and losing an additional day's work time.

Almost Best Practices

Not everyone is at the point where the forms can be e-mailed for approval. However, regardless of whether e-mail is used, an automated form with locked formulas should be employed, even if the employee then prints it out, attaches his or her receipts, and gives it to the supervisor for approval.

Reality Check for Accounts Payable

There will always be employees who don't fill out their forms correctly, don't do the appropriate coding, don't do the math (or do it wrong), use old T&E forms, and so on. Each time this happens, take the opportunity to try and educate the offending employee.

VERIFYING DATA

Background

There's a saying in T&E about "not spending a dollar to find a dime." It refers to the practice of checking every single T&E report in detail to ensure that no employee has charged something to the company that he or she is not entitled to. Some companies still feel the need to do this. This issue relates closely to corporate culture.

Best Practices

Randomly selected expense reports should be checked in detail. The percentage of reports selected can range from 5 to 25 percent, depending on the corporate tolerances. Additionally, reports from the following should be reviewed completely each time they are submitted:

- Known offenders and rogue spenders

- Any report that contains a policy violation
- Any report over a certain high-dollar amount, say $10,000

This means getting the receipts, if attached, or retrieving them if mailed in a separate envelope and verifying that all are included on the report.

Policy violations should be run by the submitter's supervisor for approval, even if the report is approved. Serious violations should be taken at least one level higher.

Almost Best Practices

Companies that want to go the spot checking route often start by verifying the data on half the reports, for example, and then working their way down to a lower level. This is a good way to start the process for those companies wanting to change the way they verify the data on the expense reports.

Reality Check for Accounts Payable

In theory, expense reports are reviewed by the submitter's supervisor and approved by this individual. The approver signs the report, indicating that he or she has checked everything and reimbursement is okay. The reality is that many supervisors don't review the reports and simply sign them without even glancing at them. This is especially true of higher-level executives as well as those in high-paying fields, such as traders, stockbrokers, and the like. Thus, sometimes checking reports is required and will not make AP popular with those whose reports are being checked.

Worst Practices

Worst practices include not checking reports at all.

HANDLING RECEIPTS

Background

When an employee completes an expense report, he or she must verify those expenses by providing receipts. The IRS guidelines require receipts for expenditures in excess of $75. However, most companies find this level a little high and require that employees submit receipts for expenditures in excess of $25.

The other issue regarding receipts is how they are sent to AP. Traditionally, receipts were attached to the expense report. Small pieces of paper of differing sizes cause problems. To get these small pieces of paper under control, some companies insist that these receipts be taped to a piece of paper before they are submitted. These pieces of paper can then be faxed to the AP department, sometimes directly into an imaging system.

At some companies, receipts are submitted along with the report so the approver can verify that the expenses are accurate. Then the receipts are shipped along with the report to AP.

Another approach is to have the receipts sent to AP in a bar-coded envelope for filing. Companies that utilize electronic T&E approaches typically employ this approach.

Best Practices

A case can be made for requiring receipts for expenditures over either $25 or $75. The $75 level has been allowable for a while, but companies have been slow to increase the requirement at their firms.

When receipts are submitted to AP, they should be sent in specially coded envelopes. They should not be attached to the reports, from which they can easily become separated.

Almost Best Practices

If receipts are not sent separately, get rid of those pesky little pieces of paper. Insist that they be taped to a larger piece of paper. Ideally, all will fit on one piece of paper. A company that sets the limit at which receipts must be submitted at either $25 or $75 should not have many little pieces of paper. Companies that set that limit at $5 (yes, there are some companies that have limits that low!) can get tons of these little receipts submitted.

Reality Check for Accounts Payable

Regardless of the dollar level set by the company, there will be employees who will insist on submitting receipts for every last cent they spend. Work to educate these employees.

Worst Practices

Worst practices include insisting that employees submit all receipts.

RESERVATIONS

Background

This is an arena that is changing rapidly even as this is being written. Until the last few years, companies routinely required employees to book their travel arrangements through preapproved travel agencies. Larger companies negotiated special rates, based on volume usage, with airlines, hotel chains, and car rental agencies.

The Internet has changed a lot of this. Employees routinely surf the Internet, finding lower airfares and hotel rates than are being offered by the corporate plan. Until recently, the prevailing wisdom was to stick with the corporate rate because, overall, the company gained more, due largely to the volume discounts offered by such plans. That view is starting to change as some companies now allow employees to take advantage of these lower rates when they find them.

The first crack in the agency system has appeared as one of the *Fortune* 500 companies has moved completely to the Internet for domestic travel. The savings? The $40 to $60 per ticket now paid to the agency.

Best Practices

This is probably most likely to change in the next few years. However, for now, the best practice is still to make reservations through company-approved agencies. They should:

- Get the lowest price
- Ensure policy compliance
- Guide employees to airlines and hotels where rates have been negotiated
- Make sure unused tickets are given proper treatment

Almost Best Practices

Almost best practices include allowing employees to take advantage of lower rates found on the Internet.

Reality Check for Accounts Payable

If the company policy requires use of an agency or certain airlines or hotels, expect complaints from employees who find better rates.

Worst Practices

Worst practices include having no policy regarding reservations.

REIMBURSING EMPLOYEES

Background

Employee reimbursement can be handled in one of several ways. They can

- Be given a check
- Have a check mailed to their house
- Have the reimbursement included in their paycheck
- Have the reimbursement direct deposited along with payroll
- Have the reimbursement direct deposited to a bank account

This seemingly innocuous task can create havoc in AP departments that insist on using payroll-related reimbursements. A few employees use their T&E reimbursements as "mad money," not sharing this money with their spouse. These individuals will cause quite a stir if the proposal is made to either include the reimbursements in a paycheck or have the funds direct deposited to the account where the paycheck is deposited.

Best Practices

Insist that T&E reimbursements be direct deposited to an account, but allow employees to direct the funds to an account other than the one where payroll is deposited. By adding the flexibility feature, the number of arguments will be reduced. It is beyond the responsibility of AP to address the issue between spouses.

Almost Best Practices

If the company does not insist on direct deposit, checks should be mailed to the home of the employee or included in the paycheck. See the "Worst Practices" section for what can go wrong if checks are returned to the employee.

Reality Check for Accounts Payable

If employees insists on a check, look for opportunities to get them to try the direct deposit feature, for example, when reimbursement is late and the employee needs the funds.

Worst Practices

Allowing employees to pick up reimbursement checks is an extremely inefficient use of the AP staff and causes problems when checks are misplaced or picked up by secretaries. Additionally, communication snafus between executives and their secretaries sometimes lead to a request for a second check when the first is lying on someone's desk.

UNUSED TICKETS

Background

The plans of business travelers change frequently. The result is unused tickets. With paper tickets, at least travelers have the piece of cardboard to remind them that the ticket was not used and can be either exchanged for another ticket or refunded. With e-tickets, this reminder is not available. Since many business travelers now purchase nonrefundable tickets, they are then faced with a ticket that can be used only against future travel and not refunded. Thus, it is necessary to keep track of these tickets.

Even if the ticket can be refunded, it is necessary that someone take the necessary steps to get the refund. Travel agents should help get these refunds.

Best Practices

A formal procedure should be put in place to handle unused tickets. American Express says that more than 4 percent of e-tickets issued by corporate travel departments go unused. Fortunately, new systems have emerged to track unused e-tickets and even process refunds; however, many companies are unaware of these systems. Large companies can take advantage of this new software.

Almost Best Practices

Have someone in the travel office track the status of unused tickets and send reminders to travelers who have them.

Reality Check for Accounts Payable

Unused tickets will be around as long as company employees travel. Find some system to track them; otherwise, even the most conscientious travelers will forget about them.

Worst Practices

Worst practices include doing nothing. These tickets will go unused, taking the company's cash right down the drain with them.

CASE STUDY

Making the Most of Direct Deposit

Fair Isaac Corporation has enjoyed a 95 percent or better participation in its direct deposit program. Thus, its employees are accustomed to not receiving a check. "Most of our workforce travels and incurs reimbursable expenses at least occasionally," says David Warren, the company's AP manager. "It has long been a source of complaints that we were unable to also give employees direct deposit for expense reimbursement," he explains.

The company was receiving requests from vendors to be paid either by wire transfer or through the ACH. Fair Isaac began searching for a quick solution. "We wanted to get a 'pretty good' solution in place quickly," says Warren, "rather than a more complete and expensive solution several years later."

He worked with a programmer and, where needed, several other employees. He talked to other companies in similar positions that had already implemented solutions. The company decided to use the standard Oracle payment processing to generate an output file and standard communication software and modem to send an ASCII file to the bank. An hour after the file is sent, he contacts the bank and downloads a results file. He says that throughout the process the company received good support from both BankAmerica and Oracle.

To test the new approach before going live company-wide, 20 volunteers were recruited from the finance department. The company ran test transactions for five weeks. These tests were for one cent plus any actual expense reimbursements. The company then added several dozen frequent traveler volunteers, and less than six months after the initial discussion, the system was introduced.

Initially, the company continued to provide the standard paper remittance advice for T&E reimbursements. It routed these through interoffice mail. When employees—especially those who traveled a good deal—complained, the company developed an e-mail notification system.

Application forms were also improved. They are now available on the Web. Warren hopes to eventually send the file to the bank via the Internet with the confirmation from the bank coming through e-mail. Is the program a success? "We currently have around 65 percent of our employee expense reimbursements using employee direct deposit," explains Warren. "We have had occasional problems with direct deposit delivery. However, the requests for replacement checks vastly exceed the requests for direct deposit replacements." The numbers speak for themselves.

CASE STUDY

TransUnion's Successful Low-Tech, Low-Budget T&E Solution

Like many other companies, TransUnion was saddled with a homegrown and inefficient T&E system. Set procedures were far from best practice, and management was unwilling to invest significant amounts of money to fix the process. Beth Massey, cash disbursements manager, was determined to remedy the situation, however. At a recent conference, she explained how she revamped the process using a low-budget/low-tech approach involving spreadsheets via e-mail, direct deposit, and a strict compliance policy.

THE WAY THEY WERE

With 900 frequent travelers in both the United States and Canada, the company had two full-time employees processing T&E. The company used PeopleSoft Financials and Human Resources. It is a Microsoft shop with Groupwise e-mail system. Ninety percent of the travelers were on direct deposit for reimbursement and had their money three days after the receipt of their e-mailed expense report. Massey encouraged direct deposit by processing those reports daily. Employees requesting a check were not given a guarantee as to when they would be paid. TransUnion did 100 percent audits on the back end of the process.

Many of the following *worst* practices are not exclusive to TransUnion:

- Many unauthorized expense report forms were used.
- Incomplete and incorrect forms were submitted. (Rather than using the forms provided by Massey, field personnel saved a few dollars by creating their own to look like the "official" forms.)
- Multiple expense reports were submitted at the same time.

The result was chaos. For starters, Massey says that a prior quality initiative removed control and field management accountability. Subsequently, there were an increasing number of policy violations by the travelers, for which AP—which did not have control of many aspects of the T&E function—was held accountable. She says that this resulted in an ongoing poor relationship between travelers and AP. In addition, there was constant pressure to reduce the cycle time.

DESPERATELY SEEKING SOLUTIONS

She quickly discovered that outsourcing would be more expensive than their internal solution and would audit only 10 percent of the reports. To use the PeopleSoft T&E module would require an upgrade and an intranet, both costly. Finally, she simply could have hired two more people to handle T&E. That solution was not satisfactory from the cost standpoint, however.

Massey's solution was a combination of several low-tech initiatives, including

- A direct deposit marketing initiative
- Development of an Excel expense report
- Systematic communication of policy to violators

Massey had a dream team of regional operations, sales, audit, and AP to back her up. She had sponsorship from the CFO and set a goal of the same or better turnaround with management approval. "Luckily," she says, "the sales force had just purchased laptops for the salespeople." Thus, using the Excel form while they are on the road is not a problem.

MISSION POSSIBLE

Massey says that the solution had to use minimal information technology (IT) resources or it would not have been implemented. Likewise, it could not cost more than the current solution. It had to be easy to use and implement. Finally, she was determined to take the onus off AP for matters beyond its control. The solution had to make the traveler and manager accountable.

Her solution has all the right stuff. She has inserted a secret code so the AP staff will know when they receive an expense report whether it is their form or a reproduction. The form has warnings for information necessary to process and cannot be sent with the warnings showing—they must first be fixed. The traveler routes the report via e-mail to the manager for approval.

The manager sends an approval e-mail to AP with the report attached. As soon as AP receives a signed original with receipts, they input the information and travelers get their money. Currently, the company is auditing about one third of all reports.

Massey concedes that she still takes paper expense reports from a few technically challenged individuals—a few mailroom workers and one senior executive. She hopes to implement the e-mail process for less frequent travelers.

T&E Odyssey

Now, at TransUnion, travelers can prepare their expense reports anywhere with a laptop. As soon as travelers connect to e-mail, they can route their report to the manager or designated approver. The traveler is held accountable for completing the form in compliance with policy, and the manager is accountable for ensuring policy compliance.

Massey says the key to improving the T&E system is to "do the right thing." This means

- Having executive sponsorship
- Including frequent travelers on the team devising the changes to the existing system
- Making sure that the solutions are simple and cost effective
- Running a pilot until you are sure the solution works

Those responsible for T&E who wish to improve their own system will benefit by emulating some of Massey's strategies.

CASE STUDY

Follow IBM's Lead: 21 Steps to an Award-Winning T&E Process

When Mike Gearing, IBM's international travel operations manager, told a group of business executives that IBM's increases in costs for both airfare and hotels in the year 2000 were substantially less than those experienced overall by industry, he had their attention. Speaking at the Institute of Management and Administration (IOMA) Advanced Accounts Payable Institute, Gearing explained how IBM achieved the enviable cost goals it now enjoys for T&E.

OVERVIEW

To put it bluntly, IBM spends a lot of money on the travel and entertainment expenses of its employees handling company business. The company has approximately 2.2 million travel-related transactions, which account for over $1 billion of spending. The company encourages credit card use, and 83 percent of the transactions are paid for in that manner. The remainder are reimbursed to the employees through payroll. Since 1993, the group processing T&E has

- Improved productivity 83 percent
- Improved customer satisfaction 90 percent
- Reduced the cycle time from two weeks to two days

Best of all, in 2000

- When hotel costs in industry rose by approximately 18 percent, IBM held its increases to slightly over 5 percent.
- When airfares rose approximately 4 percent, IBM managed to reduce its air-related expenses by just over 7 percent.

GOALS

Never satisfied to rest on their laurels, the professionals at IBM have set the following strategic targets to add value through the T&E process:

- *Transaction processing.* They hope to centralize globally with a continuous focus on improvement and a Web-

140

driven move toward a 100 percent paperless environment.

- *Maintain a competitive cost advantage.* The company hopes to accomplish this through global agreements and a continued selective outsourcing to take advantage of technology advances of the company's suppliers.
- *Provide superior customer support 24/7/365.* By demanding superior service from its service providers by focusing on e-business bases and establishing a call center for everyone, the company will be well on its way to achieving this goal.
- *Establish leadership in knowledge management.* By doing this, the company hopes to enhance process control and compliance and provide contract negotiation support. It also hopes to establish information warehouses to assist in the accomplishment of its goal.

Like many other companies, IBM has a T&E policy. Highlights include:

Reimbursement Policy
- 100% electronic
- Reasonable and actual
- Meal limits set in United States
- Per diems used for non-U.S. meals

Mandated Suppliers
- Corporate charge card
- Travel agency
- Car rental agency
- Hotel properties

Policy Compliance
- Monitored through Web-based claim application
- Up-front policy verification

- Increased visibility to employees and managers and recommended courses of action for exceptions

Supplier Data Feeds

- Charge card data—prefill expense reports
  - Electronic receipts
  - Supplier information
  - Improved data integrity
- Travel agency data
  - Low-cost air fare reporting
  - Independent agency audit
- Hotel folios
  - Breakdown of hotel cost into reimbursable categories

Exception Approval and Reporting

- Monthly Web-based reports at both the employee and organizational level showing:
  - Summary of spending and trending
  - Granular drill-down capability to the transaction level

Policy Exceptions

- Nonuse of the designated travel agency
- Nonuse of a negotiated hotel property
- Nonuse of the designated car rental agency
- Nonuse of lowest-cost airfare
- Expenses over the limit

IMPLEMENTATION TOOLS

While the goals established for the company are noteworthy, they are also intimidating. How can anyone accomplish the goals IBM set for itself? The answer is one step at a time. By judiciously working to eliminate the manual paper process, IBM has accomplished much of what it desires. Specifically, it

- Established an electronic submission and approval process
- Assigned account codes
- Set up an electronic notification system
- Provided online documentation and education support
- Began using imaging for records retention
- Set up a single processing system for U.S. travelers
- Gave management and employees online query capabilities
- Mandated the use of a single travel agency
- Required charge card usage and direct pay
- Made advances available only on the card
- Set up a voice response unit for employees to check claim status
- Set up a payment status check via the Intranet
- Raised the limit for miscellaneous receipts to $75
- Accepted electronic receipts for air and car rentals
- Began using data mining technologies
- Established global contracts
- Started accepting electronic hotel portfolio information via the Internet
- Began using the Internet for management reporting
- Began using an online travel reservation system
- Began prepopulating employee expense reports via the Web
- Began having exception approvals handled via the Web

HOW THE PROCESS WORKS

This all sounds very high-tech, and you may be wondering how it works in real life. Gering explained the process.

Step 1: The employee submits an expense report via the Web.

Step 2: Eighty-seven percent of those reports are sent from the employee's desktop to the server to be system audited.

Step 3: Thirteen percent (the exceptions) are sent to the manager for approval.

Step 4: The manager approves or rejects.

Step 5: Claim is sent to a tax/exception analyst (if applicable).

Step 6: Reimbursement is paid to the corporate card.

Step 7: A monthly report is sent to management.

KEYS TO SUCCESS

Gering says that the T&E team manages continuous process improvements by understanding the business and the needs of the customer. They continually evaluate the end-to-end process, looking for potential improvements.

The company does not underestimate the value of people in the process. It recognizes their contributions and empowers its staff. Cross-functional teams are the way the work gets done. Gering also emphasized that the company tried to enhance the skills of the people who worked for it, focusing on their roles as change agents and project managers. He warned the group not to underestimate the resistance they could expect whenever any new change is introduced.

He suggested that the biggest successes were achieved by focusing on

- Optimization (what's right for IBM overall)
- Reducing cycle time
- Making solutions end-user friendly (keep it simple)
- The right set of metrics
- Benchmarking frequently
- Leadership 24 hours a day

IBM's award-winning T&E process did not happen overnight. The changes and processes discussed by Gering were implemented over several years—and the company will probably continue to find ways to improve the process. If you are looking at your existing system and thinking "We'll never be that good," you are approaching T&E reengineering from the wrong angle. You have to crawl before you can walk. So study the IBM strategies and then pick a few that will work in your company and get started. Before you know it, you will have implemented them and will be back to the list to find a few more.

CASE STUDY

How Zurich America Developed Its Own Electronic T&E Report

While most T&E managers would love to have an electronic expense reporting process, not everyone has the allocated funds to purchase the fancier ones currently on the market. But it doesn't mean you can't create your own! Zurich America Insurance Company was one such firm. It owns a number of other insurance companies and runs a shared service center. When one of Zurich's companies developed its own electronic expense report, Zurich knew it had the backbone to develop such a system. Speaking at a recent conference, Dan Lyjak, the company's senior accounting operations manager, explained how the company created and improved its electronic T&E system without using outside software.

145

BACKGROUND

Like many other companies using a manual T&E process, there were numerous problems. Lyjak enumerated a few of them:

- The manual process led to time delays and mathematical errors.
- Lack of automated workflow for tracking submitted expense reports often led to confusion as to exactly where the report was. Lyjak noted that numerous virtual employees had to send manual expense reports through the mail to their approving manager.
- Reimbursements through direct deposit were not nearly as high as most T&E experts recommend.
- There were complaints by internal customers about the service levels and the untimely receipt of expense reimbursements.

Thus, when the folks at the shared service center stumbled across the electronic form, they were ready to take action.

WHAT IS ZURICH'S T&E SYSTEM?

Zurich uses SAP as its accounting software, so it was important that the new system integrate easily with SAP. Here's how Lyjak describes the new T&E software. It

- Is an Excel template and is used for business-related travel expenses
- Uses Microsoft Visual Basic macros
- Interfaces with Lotus Notes
- Uploads the data into SAP via BAPI coding

Setup

Employees must set themselves up in the new system. This has to be done only once for each employee. Each employee initializes his or her form with personal information, including

- The SAP vendor number, which is on the employee's check stub or direct deposit receipt
- Approver's name, including the Lotus Notes e-mail address
- Cost center number

Using the Software

The system prepopulates the employees' expense reports with data including dates from the credit card company. The employee then enters expense report information. After all data has been entered, the employee clicks on the submit button, and the report is

- Forwarded to the approver
- Saved on the employee's computer
- Printed along with a page of receipts that must be submitted to accounts payable

Employees don't have to calculate what is owed. In fact, no math is allowed. The fields are locked, and employees cannot override the formulas. The employee takes the copy of the expense report as well as the receipt checklist and forwards both, along with copies of the receipts, to AP.

Lyjak noted several other features that helped the T&E process along. Specifically,

- Certain fields, such as purpose of the trip, must be filled in or the system will refuse to submit the expense report.
- When an employee inputs a dollar amount, the system forces other fields. The employee cannot submit the report until the system is satisfied that all required information has been completed.

- Should an approver wish to see the actual reports, the company's T&E policy allows approvers to mandate that they see copies of all receipts. Lyjak noted that few approvers took advantage of this feature.
- When an approver is satisfied with the report, the approve button is clicked, and the employee is notified that the report has been approved and forwarded to AP for payment. It is sent to a special mailbox in AP for processing.

What Happens in Accounts Payable

The report, says Lyjak, is received in AP via Lotus Notes. Key information, such as the SAP vendor number and the authorization, is verified and then posted to SAP. An AP associate posts the information with a user ID and password. When the document has been posted, a document number is generated by the system.

A second e-mail is then sent to the employee, indicating that the expense report has been posted. The SAP document number and dollar amount are also included in the e-mail.

The AP staff then matches the submitted receipts with the paid expense reports. It also randomly audits expense reports against Zurich's corporate policy.

Unusual expense reports are also reconciled. What are unusual expense reports? Those reports that have been submitted without receipts or with miscellaneous items fall into this category.

Finally, a report for management is prepared on a quarterly basis showing the audit findings.

Advantages of the New Process

The new process provides management with reports broken down by categories requested by management. This includes sorting the data by employee or by purpose of trip. The process also allows AP to provide employees with an up-to-date status report of their expense reports and streamlines the process by taking advantage of e-mail capabilities. Most importantly, processing time has been reduced, allowing the company to

- Have a four-day turnaround time once the report is received by AP
- Eliminate manual entry into SAP
- Eliminate manual mathematical errors
- Enlist more employees to use direct deposit
- Allow AP to monitor unusual expense reports

Lyjak reports that approximately 85 percent, or 5,000, reports are now submitted electronically each month. He also set up an online simulator for initial users to try out the new system.

Process Drawbacks

Many AP professionals would love to have the system described by Lyjak. Yet, he is not completely satisfied. Lyjak says he would like the initial setup to be a little more intuitive. Currently, the system does not allow automatic linking of corporate credit card charges, nor does it have automatic links to a hierarchy to assign an approver.

THE NEXT GENERATION

Not one to rest on his laurels, Lyjak has a wish list for the future. He hopes to

- Have preapproved company travel establish a travel accrual

149

- Have a corporate credit card linked to a Web-enabled expense report
- Have payments made directly to the credit card company for the balance due on the card
- Have expense report receipts imaged into Web expense reports

What Zurich America has shown is that it is possible to have a fairly sophisticated T&E expense reporting process using existing technology. Virtually every company has Excel, and most have e-mail. A few AP departments will have a staff member with the programming capability described by Lyjak. Those that don't will have to rely on their Information Technology (IT) staff. In either event, emulating Zurich America's approach is possible. By following the approach described here, those with an antiquated, paper-based, manual T&E process will be able to transform their procedures into a state-of-the-art operation.

7

Regulatory Issues

There are a few regulatory issues that tend to end up in the Accounts Payable (AP) department. In this chapter, we investigate

- 1099s
- Sales and use tax
- Unclaimed property

1099s

Background

1099s are the forms used by companies to report to the IRS income paid to independent contractors. They are typically issued each January with a copy going to the independent contractor in question. The rules governing what must be reported, the timing of that reporting, and who can be paid on a 1099 (versus a W-2) are intricate. The IRS establishes the rules, and companies must conform to the rules or be subject to fines and penalties.

Some independent contractors would prefer that their income not be reported to the IRS and will go to great lengths to avoid providing their Taxpayer identification number (TIN) to vendors.

Best Practices

Before a vendor is set up as a new vendor in the master vendor file, a W-9 should be obtained. This can be part of the welcome packet and/or vendor application, if the company uses one. It is imperative that this be obtained before payment is made.

The IRS periodically updates its forms, so companies that issue 1099s—and virtually every company must—should review the forms they use annually.

As this book goes to press, the IRS is about to launch a TIN matching program. This will allow companies to verify names and TINs of independent contractors prior to issuing 1099s. The advantage of the matching program is that companies can avoid time-consuming reissue work by only issuing 1099s with completely correct information. However, there have been several delays in launching the program, so it remains to be seen when this will be available for broad use.

One of the productivity enhancements available as a result of the Internet is the ability to send 1099s to recipients electronically. In order to do this, permission must be obtained from the recipient. Recipients must also demonstrate that they can access the electronic statement. Of course, the best time to get this consent is upfront when the W-9 is obtained. Whether or not it is obtained at that time, try and get the consent needed.

It should be noted that payments to independent contractors should be made through AP and not payroll. Even though the lion's share of these payments goes to people who most view as employees of sorts, the payments are *not* payroll payments. Making payments through payroll can result in no 1099 being issued.

Once the IRS has the online TIN matching program up and running, TINs should be verified before the first payment is released to the contractor. While honest mistakes do happen, it is easier to get them corrected when you know where the contractor is and you have some influence over the situation.

If forms from an outside vendor are used, order your forms in November to avoid delays. This is one of those specialty functions that some companies choose to outsource.

Almost Best Practices

If the W-9 with the TIN is not obtained when the vendor is set up in the master vendor file, it should be obtained before the check is cut. By making it part of the policy and procedures of the AP department, the problem is nipped in the bud.

If the software used by the company does not have this ability or the company does not wish to be so stringent with its contractors, a policy of not releasing the check (i.e., mailing it to the recipient) until the W-9 is obtained is a reasonable alternative.

While under certain conditions it is possible to take TIN information verbally, it is much better to get it in writing, especially from those contractors who are reluctant to provide it.

Reality Check for Accounts Payable

Even if the company has a written policy of not paying vendors until W-9s are provided, AP will often find itself in the middle of a battle with a vendor who does not want to give the required tax information. Occasionally, management (especially if egged on by purchasing) will side with the vendor and demand to know why AP is being so unreasonable, or simply order AP to make the payment.

In these circumstances, AP can and should point out that if the required information is not provided, the company may be liable for the taxes owed by the vendor as well as subject to certain penalties. Additionally, it should be pointed out that if the vendor is reluctant to provide tax information before a payment is made, when the company has maximum leverage, it is unlikely that the vendor will give the data at year end, when the company is not in the driver's seat.

If forced to issue the payment after pointing out these concerns, AP should, at a minimum, document the conversations in a memo to the file. Ideally, the manager who is insisting on the payment should sign off on the memo. Why is this so important? At some later point, if the IRS discovers the problem and fines the company, the manager in question will conveniently forget about his or her order to issue the payment without the W-9. When the finger pointing starts, it's going to be AP under fire, and the department will need to be able to document that it did what it was supposed to do.

Worst Practices

Worst practices include waiting until January to make a list of all the payments made in the prior year to possible independent contractors and then trying to get all the W-9s filled out and the 1099s issued.

SALES AND USE TAX

Background

Sales tax is a tax on the retail sale of tangible personal property. It is important to note that it should be paid only on retail sales. It is also charged on certain services. Use tax is a little more complicated. It is charged by many (but not all) states on the "privilege of storing." In this case, storage means the purchaser's holding or controlling property brought in from out of state that is not intended for resale. Generally speaking, if goods are to be used for demonstration or display, they are not subject to use tax. The rules for what is and is not subject to use tax are very complicated and vary from state to state. It is imperative that the AP professionals responsible for sales and use tax learn what their state rules are.

A few companies have no formal policies and procedures for the sales and use tax responsibility. An auditor who finds a company in noncompliance is likely to be more sympathetic to a company that has a policy in place than one who has ignored the issue. The existence of a policy indicates that the company intends to pay its sales and use taxes, even if it does not always do it correctly. The lack of a formal policy implies that the company has no plan to pay. Thus, the existence of a policy is a company's first defense against an aggressive tax collector.

Even those with a policy need to revise and update it periodically, as the laws continually change. Finally, there is one last reason to have a policy in place—the communication that goes on among states and among the different taxing authorities within one state. Many in the field believe this information is freely exchanged. Once a company is hit for back payments and penalties, the likelihood is that other taxing authorities will come knocking at their door.

Best Practices

Obviously, the best practice is to have procedures in place to routinely monitor the company's sales and use tax compliance. This can be done in AP, although it is sometimes done in the tax department.

Almost Best Practices

A weak policy is better than no policy. If an auditor finds that the company has no formal policy or procedures in place, it will not look kindly on the company.

If the company is not in compliance, hire an expert to help get the company in compliance. Do not wait until the state finds you. Periodically, the states announce amnesty programs. Take advantage if you are not already in compliance.

Reality Check for Accounts Payable

This is one of those functions, like unclaimed property, that often gets swept under the rug. While AP cannot force the company to get in compliance, it can bring the issue to management's attention.

Worst Practices

Worst practices include

- Ignoring the sales and use tax issues
- Not checking employees' travel and entertainment (T&E) reports for items that might be subject to sales and use tax withholding
- Not checking purchases made on p-cards to ensure that the appropriate sales and/or use tax was withheld

UNCLAIMED PROPERTY

Background

Property holders must turn over unclaimed property to the states. The process is commonly referred to as *escheat*. While most people realize that bank accounts, life insurance premiums, and dividends must be escheated, many don't realize that uncashed checks (including payroll) and credits must also be turned over after the appropriate dormancy period. A few companies write off the balances related to uncashed checks to miscellaneous income and never turn the funds over to the states.

It will come as no surprise to those reading this to learn that the states have been aggressively pursuing the collection of funds from all sources, especially those that come from entities that do not vote. Unclaimed property falls into this category. Not only are states increasing the number of audits—often outsourcing to third parties who are paid a percentage of what they collect—but they are also often working together. That's right, they are sharing information. In a worst-case scenario, even midsize companies could find themselves faced with unclaimed property audits from multiple states.

Should a company be found to be not in compliance, it can be assessed penalties in addition to having to turn over an estimated amount for prior years—and there is no statute of limitations.

The laws that govern unclaimed property include

- The Uniform Unclaimed Property Act of 1954
- A Supreme Court ruling in 1965
- The Uniform Unclaimed Property Act of 1981
- The Uniform Unclaimed Property Act of 1995

Best Practices

Those not in compliance need to get in compliance quickly. The easiest way to do so is to take advantage when a state offers an amnesty period, which has happened several times in the last few years. When there are amnesty periods, it is on a state-by-state basis—they don't all do it at the same time.

Assuming that there is no amnesty program, it is still better to approach the states and deal with the issue than to wait for them to find you in noncompliance. The reason for this is that they are apt to deal more leniently with those who confess their omissions than with those whom they catch avoiding the process.

Those in noncompliance are advised to consult with an attorney with escheat experience to help guide them through this arduous process.

Once a company is in compliance, it must report to each state annually. Of course, all the states do not have the same deadline—that might make the process too easy. The majority of the states have a November 1 deadline, with March 1 being the filing date for another large group of the states. These filings must be done on time, as the states typically have a penalty for late filing in addition to the fine for nonfilers!

The rules for due diligence and reporting are intricate and the task should be either

- Outsourced to specialty experts
- Assigned to an in-house expert

One of the best practices regarding uncashed checks is simple: Have as few checks left outstanding as possible. This means systematically following up on all uncashed checks on a regular basis, not just at the end of the year. Since your company is not going to get to hold onto the funds, you may as well give them to their rightful owner.

In addition to researching uncashed checks to ensure that the funds end up in the hands of the rightful property owners, companies should establish rigid procedures for their payment processes as well as other AP functions. Not only will this ensure a well-running operation, minimize (if not eliminate) duplicate payments, and make fraud more difficult, they will help the company minimize unnecessary escheatment.

Almost Best Practices

If an ongoing attempt is not made throughout the year to research uncashed checks, at a minimum this research should be done in the weeks before the filings are done.

Reality Check for Accounts Payable

For a while there was talk of a business-to-business (B2B) escheat exclusion, the theory being that an uncashed check from one business to another probably represented a duplicate payment. While a few states did enact such legislation, it is effective only if both the payee and the payor are in states either without escheat laws or with the B2B exclusion. Thus, most professionals now realize that, with a few exceptions, the exclusion is virtually worthless. Those counting on our lawmakers to save them from this task were woefully disappointed.

Worst Practices

Worst practices include not escheating. While it may seem like a smart financial move, adding to the bottom line, it is only a matter of time before the practice catches up with the company, and—like everything else in life—it will happen at the worst possible time. For some companies, this occurs when they are acquired by a larger company that follows the rules and escheats as it should. For others, the auditors show up in a lean year when everyone is struggling to keep the bottom line out of the red. Then the fines and penalties turn what could have been a marginal year into a losing one.

CASE STUDY

How to Avoid Sales and Use Tax
Audit Disasters

How seriously does your company take its sales and use tax oversight responsibilities? Speaking at a recent conference,

Deloitte & Touche's manager Brian Kelleher recommended three approaches that would prevent such a catastrophe. He spoke about a managed compliance agreement, a reverse sales and use tax audit, and automation.

MANAGED COMPLIANCE AGREEMENT

Kelleher warns that a managed compliance agreement must be negotiated in advance with the state. He calls it a simplified method for reporting sales and use tax on purchases. Here's how it works:

- In most cases, the company enters into an agreement with the state for a period of three years.
- The company should obtain a direct-pay permit from the state and then make its purchases tax free.
- Each month, the company computes an effective tax rate and then remits to the state the tax based on the computed effective rate.

There are many benefits to this approach. For starters, cash flow is increased; and it minimizes overpayments and underpayment, both of which can cause problems for a corporation. Companies using this approach say that compliance is greatly simplified. They also praise the reduced audit and compliance costs.

REVERSE SALES AND USE TAX AUDITS

As those familiar with the myriad sales and use tax laws are well aware, it is very easy to overpay sales or use tax. The rules are complicated and constantly change, and personnel handling the function often leave. Some of the compliance tools used by corporations are not completely effective either.

Thus, some companies hire outside experts to come in

and identify refund opportunities. These same experts will also pinpoint potential areas where the company might have an exposure. In both of these cases, the company can take one of two courses of action: Either file for a refund, to pay excess taxes owed, or simply fix the problem to ensure future compliance.

Kelleher says reverse sales and use tax audits have three phases: identify, quantify, and secure tax refunds.

Many companies that handle reverse audits for companies do so for a percentage of the savings. A company that undertakes a reverse sales and use tax audit benefits in several ways. In addition to the improved cash flow, it also receives recommendations to improve compliance and has its staff educated, so mistakes can be avoided in the future.

AUTOMATION

Technology is the ideal solution to nitpicky technical issues, and sales and use tax compliance certainly falls into that category. Several companies have developed software to assist in that endeavor. Some of the products on the market today include Vertex, Taxware, and CorpSales (a Deloitte & Touche product).

ADDITIONAL RESOURCES

Due to the constantly changing regulations, which vary by state and even by county, many AP professionals subscribe to publications to keep them on top of the issue. One of the best-known publications is BNA's *Sales and Use Tax Rates and Forms* (to find additional information about BNA's products go to *www.bnasoftware.com/soft/surfabout.html*).

Those who wish to educate their staff about sales and use tax will find the sessions given by the Sales Tax Institute of great interest. To find out when the next seminars will be given, go to *www.salestaxinstitute.com/*.

CONCLUSION

How serious an issue is this? Just ask Dennis Kozlowski, Tyco International's CEO who was charged with cutting illegal deals to avoid more than $1 million in taxes on valuable old paintings. Here's what New York District Attorney Robert M. Morgenthau had to say about the Tyco situation: "The state and the city are in a fiscal crisis. For someone who was so highly paid to fail to pay over a million dollars in sales tax is a serious crime. There will be zero tolerance in New York for tax fraud and tax evasion, and I hope the federal government will take a similar view."

CASE STUDY

A Typical Company's Unclaimed Property Experience

Unclaimed property is supposed to be turned over to the state. Each state has different guidelines and requirements, making the process difficult for AP professionals whose companies operate in or do business with companies that operate in more than one state. To clarify the process and some of the misconceptions surrounding unclaimed property issues, Karen Anderson, a vice president of Unclaimed Property Recovery & Reporting, Inc. (UPRR) shared her expertise. Her advice will get even the escheat novice headed down the right path.

162

HOW IT BEGINS

Most AP professionals get involved in unclaimed property in one of the following ways:

- The state sends a notice saying that the company needs to file an unclaimed property report or that the state is sending unclaimed property auditors to the company.
- While attending a seminar, they discover that the company has unclaimed property obligations.
- The firm that recently purchased the company requires its subsidiaries to comply with unclaimed property laws.
- The company complies with all applicable laws, including escheat.

Whatever the cause, AP professionals often find themselves thrust into reviewing unclaimed property obligations with little warning.

BACKGROUND

As most AP professionals are well aware, escheatment is a requirement that all unclaimed property be turned over to the state. The specifics of when and how vary from one state to another. Included in the definition of *unclaimed property* are uncashed checks and credit balances. After an uncashed check sits on the books for a period of time, some companies pocket the funds, writing it off as miscellaneous income. This money should be turned over to the state in a process referred to as unclaimed property or escheat.

GOING THROUGH THE ESCHEAT PROCESS

For those who have no unclaimed property procedures in place, getting started can seem like an overwhelming task. Anderson recommends a very methodical approach, as follows:

Step 1: Assess the Situation

- Review past compliance.
- Has the company ever reported unclaimed property? If so, what, when, and where?
- Has the company ever been subject to a state unclaimed property audit? If so, what were the results and what states were part of the audit?
- Are there any subsidiaries to be included?
- Has the company made any recent acquisitions that should be included?

Step 2: Determine Eligible Property

- Does your company have some of the property types covered by most states? These include:
  - Vendor checks
  - Payroll checks
  - Customer credits
  - Refunds
  - Gift certificates
  - Common or preferred stock
  - Long-term debt
- What states are represented among the names and addresses to be reported?
- If this is an initial filing, what about years that may not be on the books?

Step 3: Perform the Due Diligence

- What due diligence is required by state? Specifically, focus on
  - Minimum dollar amount
  - Timing
  - Method
  - Content notice
- What about operational due diligence? This might include developing a strategy to minimize unclaimed

property liability and reviewing potentially reportable items.

- Prepare the due diligence letter. This should include the following important elements:
  - Response deadline
  - Identification number and amount
  - Property type/reason
  - Instructions for claiming

Step 4: Prepare Reports and Remittances

- Identify due dates for states.
- Prepare a cover sheet with signature.
- Use the proper medium (paper, diskette, etc.).
- Use the proper report format.
- Include the remittance (check, wire transfer, etc.).

Step 5: Filing Reports and Remittances

- File on time to avoid penalties and interest.
- Get extensions in writing. Only some states will grant them.

Step 6: Follow-up and Reconcilement

- Reconcile the general ledger to detail.
- Reconcile paid items to the appropriate accounts/divisions.
- File any necessary holder reimbursement claims with the states.
- Establish a filing system for reports and work papers.

Step 7: Celebrate

OTHER IMPORTANT INFORMATION

Anderson points out several other useful facts, such as

- Forty-one states have fall deadlines. The remaining nine states have spring deadlines.

- AP professionals can expect more audits as state governments look for ways to generate income.
- AP professionals should also be aware that many firms are performing audits for several states at the same time.
- Never volunteer extra information during an audit. Give the auditors the documents they ask for and nothing more. There is no reason to give them ammunition for an audit for a different state.

8

Cash Management

As accounts payable (AP) moves from being a largely transactional profession to a more analytical one, topics not normally associated with this group are creeping in. The most successful AP departments realize that they must take a cash management view. In this chapter, we take a look at

- Taking early payment discounts
- Payment status information for vendors
- Bank accounts and fraud
- Other cash management–related initiatives

TAKING EARLY PAYMENT DISCOUNTS

Background

Early payment discounts are the concessions vendors sometimes offer their customers in order to entice them to pay early. The most common payment term to incorporate these inducements is 2/10 net 30. It offers customers a 2 percent discount if they pay the invoice within 10 days of receiving the invoice instead of on the 30th day. There are several problems

167

that often arise in connection with the early payment discount. The first relates to when the clock starts ticking. Usually, the customer and the vendor have a different idea of when the timing starts: The customer believes that the time starts when the invoice hits the AP department, while the vendor starts counting on the date on the invoice.

Companies sometimes have a difficult time processing invoices in a timely enough manner to qualify for the early payment discount. Let's face it, 10 days isn't a lot of time when

- AP has to receive and log in the invoice.
- A copy of the invoice must be sent to the appropriate person for approval.
- The approver has to review the invoice, approve it, and return it to AP.
- The associate in AP has to process the invoice and schedule it for payment.
- The check has to be printed and signed in the appropriate check run, which can be as infrequent as once a week.

So, companies sometimes stretch the period and take the discount a few days after the early payment discount period really has ended.

There are companies whose sole business is collecting unearned discounts. The amount of money is not huge, but the amount of effort involved in researching these amounts when the collectors come calling should make those taking the unearned discounts think twice.

Best Practices

In theory, companies should perform an analysis to determine if it is financially advantageous to pay early and take the discount. However, as this is written, interest rates are so low that such an analysis is a waste of time. When rates are higher, the analysis is an absolute requirement.

The goal—assuming that it is financially profitable to take the discount—should be to take all discounts for which the company qualifies. Many companies stretch the early payment term for a few days and will take the discount up until, for example, the 15th day.

Whatever the policy regarding taking discounts after the discount period has ended, it should be formalized and in writing.

Payments—especially large ones—that involve an early payment discount should be flagged to ensure that they receive priority handling so that discounts are not lost.

Almost Best Practices

Some large companies do not routinely accept the terms offered by their vendors. Instead, they set their own terms, including discount periods, and require vendors to accept them. Most vendors do accept the terms in order to do business with these firms.

Reality Check for Accounts Payable

Vendors do not appreciate customers who take early payment discounts and then do not pay within the discount period. Some will try and collect the unearned discounts, and others will eventually raise prices to cover this charge.

A few vendors take this issue so seriously that they will accrue the unearned discounts, and when they reach a certain level they put the customer on credit hold. No AP professional wants to be responsible for getting the company put on credit hold by a key supplier. So, if your company wants to take the discounts regardless of when the invoice is paid, make sure that the policy is approved by senior management and is in writing. This is not a decision to be made lightly, nor is it one AP should make on its own.

Worst Practices

Worst practices include

- Having no formal policy regarding taking early payment discounts
- Taking all discounts even when payments are made after the discount period and/or after the due date. Some companies pay 60 days late and still take the early payment discount, which antagonizes vendors.

PAYMENT STATUS INFORMATION FOR VENDORS

Background

One of the problems for AP is the endless phone calls from vendors inquiring about the status of their invoices. Most want to know either why they have not been paid or when they will be paid. These calls are disruptive and do not add any value to the payment function. Worse, they require AP to research the particular invoice and return the call. If there were some simple way to share this information with vendors, the number of phone calls coming into AP could be reduced.

Best Practices

First, good policies and procedures with regard to the entire invoice-handling process will ensure not only that payments get made in a timely manner, but the number of phone calls inquiring about payment status will decline.

Most vendors are perfectly happy with a self-service application when it comes to following up on their invoices. Giving vendors a place to find the information regarding payment and invoice status will make a serious dent in the number of phone calls coming into the department. There are two ways that work well:

1. Interactive voice response (IVR)
2. The Internet

IVR units allow the vendor to call a phone number and in response to several voice prompts get the status of their invoices and the date the check will be cut.

Similarly, the same information can be put on the Internet. With the appropriate user IDs, passwords, and invoice numbers, vendors can check on the status of their invoices and anticipated payments.

With both of these approaches, not only can the vendor determine the information it needs, it can also send along a second invoice if it realizes that you have not received their invoice.

Almost Best Practices

While not the best approach in the world, some companies that have not found a way to institute best practices try one or more of the following:

- Assign one or more people to the task of answering these calls, researching the invoice status, and replying to the vendor with this information.
- Limit the time of day when someone in AP will answer vendor inquiries.
- Research and respond to only those invoice inquiries for payments that are more than 30 days past due.
- Set up an e-mail address where vendors can send inquiries.

- Refuse to respond to those vendors who continually call before the payment date to see if the invoice has been received and that there are no problems.

Reality Check for Accounts Payable

No matter how good the company's payment practices and information-sharing facilities, the calls will still come. If the company has implemented some of the best practices and a key vendor calls with an invoice inquiry, someone in AP will have to respond. However, he or she can gently walk the vendor through the payment status process, either on an IVR or on the Internet.

Worst Practices

Worst practices include having whoever answers the phone research the payment or invoice status that the caller has inquired about.

BANK ACCOUNTS AND FRAUD

Background

Crooks looking to defraud companies have found numerous ways around the safeguards put in place. One of the more common ways check fraud occurred in the past was for the thief to call the Treasury department and ask for wire instructions in order to make a payment. Of course, the thief did not really intend to send the company a payment; he simply wanted the company's bank account number. With the account number and the CEO's signature from the annual financial statements, the thief had all the information needed to forge checks.

Another approach was to order an item, overpay, and then wait for the refund check to arrive with all the information needed—the bank account number and a copy of an authorized signer's signature. These are just a few of the more common ways thieves commit check fraud. Companies wanting to protect themselves against these and other types of check fraud must establish their bank accounts with care.

Of course, the real way to get away from check fraud is to eliminate paper checks. Many companies are attempting that, especially in conjunction with electronic invoicing (e-invoicing) initiatives.

Best Practices

When disbursing money,

- No checks should be written on the bank accounts used for wire transfers.
- The CEO's signature in the annual statements should *not* be his or her actual signature.
- Refunds should be written on accounts with a dollar limit on the payment amount.
- Automated clearinghouse (ACH) blocks should be put on accounts in which ACH debits are not permitted, which for most companies will be most of their bank accounts.
- Wherever possible, vendors should be paid with ACH credits.
- Positive pay should be used on all accounts.
- Accounts should be reconciled quickly—ideally every day.

Almost Best Practices

Absolutely, checking accounts should be reconciled within 30 days of receipt.

Reality Check for Accounts Payable

Expect big changes in this area in the next few years. Increasingly, companies that would not consider electronic payments at all are changing their minds. Those who find a vendor reluctant to change today should not give up. Go back to them in six months or a year and you may find that they have made the necessary changes to their accounting systems and can accommodate electronic payments. In fact, with the appropriate changes made, they may welcome the move to electronic payments. Approach the customers that are moving to e-invoicing with your proposals for making electronic payments.

Worst Practices

Worst practices include ignoring the implications of fraud that can creep into the process if adequate care is not taken with the payment process.

OTHER CASH MANAGEMENT–RELATED INITIATIVES

Background

Today, companies everywhere are focusing on cash flow. What many often overlook is that the AP department can help a company improve its cash position, not only by taking advantage of early payment discounts and timing payments, but by approaching a number of AP initiatives with care. The result will be less cash going out, which positively affects the bottom line.

Best Practices

Cash management is not something that is typically discussed in AP. This is an area where the AP manager not only can make a difference, but he or she can also use the cash management issues to stand out from the crowd and improve the image of the department. The AP manager with cash management instincts should

- Research all uncashed checks as early as 90 days. This allows the AP department to resolve escheat-type issues while the facts are still fresh and ultimately results in lower amounts to be turned over to the states as well as improved vendor relations.
- Periodically request statements from all vendors (frequency depending on level of activity) showing all outstanding activity, including credits. Collect or use all credits as quickly as possible.
- Move as many vendors as possible to electronic payment (ACH) mechanisms, significantly reducing payment-processing costs.
- Track lost discounts and the reasons those discounts were lost. Research and resolve these issues.
- Report on the issues discussed here on a periodic basis—ideally monthly. Quantify all savings.

Almost Best Practices

Because of time constraints, companies often do not have time to review the statements from all vendors. However, every vendor should be contacted at least once a year to ensure that there are no outstanding credits. If you are having trouble finding the time to do this, see if you can hire a temp to do it and then keep track of the credits found and collected. The project should more than pay for itself, making it easier to get funding the second year. Also, identify those vendors that seemed to have the most outstanding credits and try and follow up with them for additional activity after six months. Again, if you collected a significant amount the first time around, management may be a little more willing to fund your project.

If the corporate culture will not allow you to aggressively pursue vendors to entice them to accept payments electronically, try to use an electronic payment whenever a Rush check is requested.

Reality Check for Accounts Payable

Yes, the preceding steps will take additional time and you are unlikely to be given additional staff to perform them. But, ultimately, they will pay off, not only for the company with its improved bottom line, but for the AP department with a more efficient workflow.

Worst Practices

Worst practices include the following:

- The clean desk syndrome can have a negative impact on a company's cash flow and bottom line if funds are disbursed before the due date. The only silver lining to the early disbursements is that the vendor will appreciate your thoughtfulness.
- Ignoring outstanding uncashed checks until it is time to turn unclaimed property over to the states
- Ignoring laggard approvers who routinely cause the company to lose early payment discounts
- Paying before the due date

CASE STUDY

General Electric's Approach to Electronic Invoicing and Payment Processing

Like many companies, General Electric (GE) recognized the inherent inefficiencies of its paper-based payment process.

Unlike other companies, when GE decides to change something, its suppliers generally get in line and do what GE wants. Speaking at a recent conference, GE's David W. Hay explained the GE approach to e-invoicing and payment processing. While most attending did not have the same clout to implement an e-invoicing program, there were many valuable lessons to be learned from the seminar.

GE'S VISION

Hay described GE's vision for the future, which could be quite exciting for its AP department. For starters, GE believes its e-invoicing and payment processing should be purchase-order driven, including Web-enabled invoice and invoiceless settlement processes. It would also like its process to include transactional transparency that highlights status and history.

The company would like to use workflow approval for complex transactions and services. It also needs its final system to be global and have multicurrency capabilities. A virtual three-way real-time match is the goal.

The company believes that now is the time to start to develop an electronic process. Currently, 70 percent of its invoices are manual. This severely taxes its capabilities, and the company wonders if it will be able to handle its forecasted seven trillion transactions. Its manual processes are very inefficient, and the company sees the opportunity for huge cost savings.

SAVINGS OPPORTUNITIES

The company identified several savings prospects if it could move into an electronic environment. These include

- *Lost discount.* Most of its suppliers offer a discount of 1 to 3 percent for prompt pay. Currently, the company loses 77 percent of these due to processing inefficiencies. The savings attributable to attaining all of the eligible discounts on the company's estimated $45 billion annual spend is huge.

- *Reduced customer service costs.* The company's buyers spend up to 20 percent of their time answering calls about payments. This is compounded by the fact that 70 percent of the calls that come to the AP department are from internal buyers following up on payments to vendors. Clearly, this area is ripe for process improvements.
- *Eliminating the two- and three-way match.* The manual process is time consuming, leads to payment delays, and is costly considering the high mismatch rate.

GETTING STARTED

The company evaluated its invoices and discovered that 82 percent of them were for less than $2,500. It also discovered that it took anywhere from 25 to 40 days to process an invoice, 26 percent of the invoices failed the match, and 77 percent of trade discounts were missed. Since the company offers 60-day terms with an early discount available at 15 days, its existing processes made it impossible to take the discount. Many reading this may be thinking that the vendor, *not* the buyer, offers terms. That is correct, unless the buyer in question is GE, who tells its vendors what terms it will pay.

The company analyzed its defects and discovered that paper accounted for most of its problems. It analyzed its top six invoice errors by document type and found that:

- Thirty-two percent were for account number errors.
- Twenty-one percent were for receiving errors.
- Eleven percent were related to the PO.
- Ten percent were due to missing approvals.

- Six percent were attributable to advise line and quantity errors.
- Six percent had incorrect Remit-To addresses.

Clearly, the key to solving the problem lay in eliminating paper.

By preparing a detailed financial analysis, the company estimated that it could save $240 million annually if it could get a handle on its payment process so it qualified for all of its discounts. There would be additional productivity savings if it could streamline its processes so all those calls to AP would not be necessary—something that would automatically fall into place if its vendors were being paid on time!

THE SOLUTION: PART 1

For starters, the company requires a PO for everything. It then employs a variety of electronic initiatives for handling the payment piece. As you might expect, the company uses a p-card for all transactions under $2,500. This method is especially efficient at GE since the company has its own credit card program.

It uses evaluated receipt settlement (ERS) for direct materials. This approach is also referred to as pay-on-receipt or invoice-free processing. The company has certain existing electronic data interchange (EDI) relationships, which it continues to employ. Like most other professionals, Hay does not see the application disappearing despite the fact that he calls it a dinosaur.

Finally, the company expects to use a Web invoicing settlement application for approximately one third of its invoices that do not fall into one of the other categories. While each of the techniques has advantages for GE, none are perfect. He shared with the audience an interesting tidbit. Did you know that in China, execution can be a punishment for value-added tax fraud?

THE SOLUTION: PART 2

The company was looking to reduce its processing time so it could take advantage of discounts while simultaneously reducing the costs associated with the payment inquiries into AP. While the payment alternatives discussed above will make a serious dent in the problem, they do not provide the total answer. The company is also considering

- Invoicing
- Self-service invoice inquiry
- Web invoice submission
- Automatic PO-to-invoice match
- Web payment status

MEASURING SUCCESS

As might be expected, a company like GE will regularly check to see if it is meeting its goals. In the case of the new invoice match and pay process, Hay says the company measures

- *Trade discounts achieved.* It hopes to earn at least 70 percent of those available and appears to be exceeding that goal.
- *Cycle time.* In order to earn the discounts, the company set a goal of an eight-day cycle. At the time of the talk, that goal had yet to be achieved.
- *PO failure.* There was still a bit of work to be done in this area.
- *Invoices processed.* The company was right on target in this area.

Since the system had only recently been implemented, GE had achieved a remarkable amount, although it felt it had a few areas left for improvement.

9

Technology

Technology is radically changing the face of the accounts payable (AP) world. In this chapter, we'll take a look at a few of those innovations, including

- Imaging and workflow
- The Internet
- E-invoicing

The case studies at the end of this chapter, while demonstrating each of the techniques discussed, also reveal how interconnected the different technologies and approaches are with regard to AP.

IMAGING AND WORKFLOW

Background

As companies search for ways to eliminate paper from their processes as well as streamline their operations, imaging and workflow top the list of ways to achieve that goal. Imaging can be as simple as a small scanner such as the ones that many consumers have at home hooked up to their personal computers or a more complex process. That imaging process consists of

- Capture and index
- Delivery
- Storage (both online and archived)
- Retrieval

The most critical step in the procedure is the capture and indexing phase, since the other steps depend on it. Most companies that use imaging do so for a variety of reasons. They tend to see benefits in the following areas:

- Improved processing
- Improved security
- Integration
- Customer service
- Document storage

However, as with any new technology, there are some issues that need to be resolved. They include

- *Index structure.* This is not standardized, and those purchasing imaging systems should make sure that the index structure offered is one that will meet all their requirements.
- *Cost.* Although prices have dropped, this technology is still expensive by certain standards. Make sure you understand all the costs before purchasing a system. This is also important if you do not purchase your own equipment but go with the services of a third-party service provider.
- *Lack of standards.* Many experts believe that although there currently is no conformity among manufacturers, standards will emerge within the next few years. It is in the best interests of the manufacturers—especially since there does not appear to be any Microsoft-size imaging providers.

- *Legal acceptance.* Some professionals are concerned about not having an original document in case of legal action. Currently, most professionals feel confident that the best evidence rule will hold up, but it has not yet been tested at the state level in all locales. Needless to say, no one is anxious to be the test case.
- *Disaster recovery.* The issues in this arena are virtually the same as in a paper-based environment.

Once the information has been imaged, it can be forwarded to the appropriate parties using workflow. The most prominent marriage of imaging and workflow in AP occurs when it is used with invoices, first imaging them and then forwarding those images to the appropriate parties for approvals. Workflow can be programmed to include escalating approvals, thus eliminating the problems associated with recalcitrant approvers.

Best Practices

One of the easiest imaging applications for AP is getting canceled checks on a CD-ROM from the bank. From a practical standpoint, there are a number of occasions when the AP staff will find having canceled checks on a CD-ROM very helpful, as shown in the following examples:

- When a supplier calls and says a payment was not received, the AP clerk usually goes to the files, pulls the check, makes a photocopy, and then either mails or faxes it to the vendor. The check must then be refiled. This assumes, of course, that no one else has pulled that particular check and that it has been refiled. If it hasn't, the clerk must then go and find the unfiled checks. With the information on CD-ROM, the clerk is able to access the information with a few clicks of the mouse and print it.
- If the company has supplied a fax modem for the employee's computer, the copy can be automatically faxed.

The employee never has to leave his or her desk and can handle this type of request in a few seconds. The image of the check can also be copied onto the clipboard and then pasted into a memo, if that is what is required.

- Sometimes, it is not necessary to provide a copy of the check, but only to ascertain if it has been presented for payment. In these instances, it is possible to check the information as indicated above and then pass on the information verbally.

As indicated here, if invoices are imaged up front, they can be forwarded for approvals using workflow.

If e-invoicing is used, the invoices received electronically can be shared using workflow.

Travel and entertainment (T&E) expense reimbursement forms can be forwarded for approval using workflow. Similarly, receipts can be imaged, eliminating the need to save those annoying slips of paper.

Almost Best Practices

If a full-blown imaging and workflow system is not possible, AP departments can purchase small scanners for use in the department. Then, instead of making a paper copy of the invoice and sending it out for approval, a scanned copy of the invoice can be attached to an e-mail requesting approval. While this "poor man's imaging system" provides some of the benefits of a full-blown one, it does not have all the benefits of the more complicated systems.

Reality Check for Accounts Payable

The integration of e-invoicing, e-mail, and imaging systems is where this application is going at virtually all companies, although it will take a little time for this technology to find its way into smaller companies.

Worst Practices

Worst practices include not learning everything possible about imaging and workflow, assuming that it will never find its way to smaller companies. It will.

THE INTERNET

Background

It would hardly be an understatement to say that the Internet has changed the way AP is handled in virtually every company. When companies first started using the Internet, some were reluctant to give access to employees for a variety of reasons, including

- Fear that employees would abuse the technology
- Concern about viruses
- Worry about personal use

Today, virtually all AP professionals have access to the Internet, helping to make them as effective as possible.

Best Practices

There are many ways that the Internet is being used to facilitate the AP function today, such as

- Using e-mail to communicate with suppliers and other employees
- Creating an AP Web site. It should include
  - Procedures for getting invoices paid
  - Contact information for the AP department

- Forms related to AP
- Frequently asked questions (FAQs)
- T&E policy, procedures, and forms
- P-card policy and related information

- Verifying new vendors to eliminate potential fraudulent vendors
- Using the Web to provide payment status information to vendors
- Researching new products, new technologies, and new suppliers:
  - Confirming correct addresses
  - Checking UPS and FedEx tracking codes
  - Verifying zip codes
  - Viewing bill of lading (BOL) and signed receipts through freight company sites
  - Verifying tax information
  - Verifying currency conversion rates
  - Checking vendors' sites for tracking information
  - Researching regulatory information
  - Reporting independent contractors to the state
  - Looking up the licenses and status of subcontractors
  - Researching property tax bills
  - Verifying new vendors
  - Checking air rates, car rental rates, and hotels
  - Obtaining signed proofs of delivery
  - Checking vendor sites for statements and past-due invoices, where available
  - Using information to present new procedures and ideas
  - Finding additional information about suppliers
  - Locating 1099 information and company card account/transactions

- Finding floor plan financing information
- Researching outstanding balance issues with vendors

Almost Best Practices

More than a few AP departments use the Internet only for e-mail. Although this is definitely a step in the right direction, it is like using a computer as an adding machine. True, it can add numbers, but it can do a lot more, and not taking advantage of all its features leaves a lot on the table. The departments that are the most productive are the ones that use the Internet in numerous ways.

Reality Check for Accounts Payable

The applications for AP, as well as the way the Internet can be used to improve various business processes, will continue to evolve. In order to be successful on an ongoing basis, AP professionals will have to stay on top of what can be done using the Internet.

Worst Practices

Worst practices include not giving everyone in AP access to the Internet.

E-INVOICING

Background

Electronic invoicing, also referred to as e-invoicing or Web invoicing, is the electronic delivery of invoices, mostly over the Internet, to the AP department. No paper is received. The AP department forwards the invoice, via e-mail, to the person who needs to approve it. The information is then available, without further keying, to be housed on a network for data retrieval purposes.

In addition to the elimination of mountains of paper, companies like e-invoicing because

- Mistakes are reduced, as there is no need to rekey information.
- Use of easy workflow to route invoices for approval
- Cost reduction
- Difficulty in blaming AP for others' own shortcomings in processing paper

Companies have not embraced e-invoicing as much as they might have liked because of the

- Cost
- Implementation time
- Budget constraints
- Internal resistance to change
- Lack of ease of use
- Difficulty in signing up partners
- Fear

Companies interested in pursuing the e-invoicing route will base their decision on the

- Existing internal processes
- Budget
- Corporate culture
- Willingness to mandate changes both internally and externally

Best Practices

Support the use of e-invoicing wherever possible. The benefits, as described earlier, make it an approach that should be encouraged. Invoices can be

- Picked up at the supplier's Web site (seller-centric)
- Delivered by the supplier to the purchaser's Web site (buyer-centric) or
- Picked up at a consolidator site (consolidator model)

Almost Best Practices

Almost best practices include accepting invoices electronically from any vendor willing to send them, but not pursuing the practice actively.

Reality Check for Accounts Payable

As much as one would think that vendors would be rushing to invoice electronically, that is not always the case. The push has been coming more from the AP side.

Worst Practices

Worst practices include refusing to enter the e-invoicing world.

CASE STUDY

PPL Electric Offers Lessons on Setting Up an Accounts Payable Imaging Solution

Do any of your AP processors leave difficult invoices for someone else to process? Do they wait until 5 o'clock to slide problem invoices past their supervisors? Are you sick of piles of paper and rows of filing cabinets? If the answer to any or all of these questions is yes, imaging and workflow may be for you.

Brian Krom, corporate disbursements manager, shared his experiences with implementing an imaging and workflow solution at PPL Electric Utilities Corporation. First, however, is a description of why PPL wanted to move in this direction.

WHY IMAGING AND WORKFLOW

Krom enumerated seven reasons for moving to imaging and workflow:

1. *Processed efficiencies and reduced cycle times.* This was accomplished by decreasing paper handoffs, decreasing or eliminating bottlenecks, eliminating manual date stamping, reducing the delays in routing "trouble" invoices, and saving on labor costs.

2. *Improved work distribution through FIFO (first in, first out) processing.* Invoices were prioritized within or between queues, and flexibility and control were added over individual image filters.

3. *Improved monitoring, tracking, and reporting of the vouchering (workflow) and backlogs.* This was achieved through real-time count of processed and pending invoices by operator type, scan date, and the like.

4. Improved document retention, retrieval, and archiving

5. Improved customer service

6. Improved fraud control

7. A lot less storage space

Imaging makes document handling much easier; for example, Krom can now print, fax, or e-mail images directly from within the system. He says that multiple copies of documents are no longer kept, nor are there lost, misfiled, or "out" vouchers. The need to copy and mail paper documents is eliminated, as is refiling.

Krom warns that much of the labor savings throughout the process may be offset by the labor costs for invoice sorting, prepping, and scanning. He also noted that sometimes those real-time reports of pending invoices could be quite depressing.

Imaging and workflow eliminates the need to save papers and keep microfilm/fiche. However, some AP professionals must observe certain rules to meet governmental requirements. Krom summarizes the Securities and Exchange Commission (SEC) and IRS rules, but cautions that additional regulations may apply. He points out that it is not required to convert to imaging as your source document, but if you do, you must follow the regulations.

STORAGE SPACE ISSUE

Space saving is usually an issue whenever the imaging topic comes up. Krom demonstrated just how much space PPL saves. He says that the AP department fills up 82 filing cabinets each year. Each cabinet takes up eight square feet of floor space (this includes two feet of clearance to open the drawers). That's approximately 650 square feet of space each year. Trying to find something in one of these cabinets is another challenge.

The 5¼-inch optical platters used by the PPL AP department each hold 2.6 gigabytes of images. Seventeen are used for each year's information. Next year, Krom plans to upgrade to platters that can hold twice as much information.

IMPLEMENTATION

To begin with, PPL developed a business case. Tentative management approval was gained, and a vendor was selected that satisfied AP's requirements as they understood them at the time.

PPL tried to understand the software functionality and tested and experimented with it. PPL spoke with other users and even insisted on talking to the technical staff as well as the salespeople. Krom urges others to do the same. He also recommends speaking with other customers of the software vendor.

PPL then mapped out the current process. This mapping was more difficult and took longer than expected, but PPL learned a lot from the process. With the current information under its belt, PPL designed and mapped the new process. When gaps in the process were identified, the company then had to decide whether to change the process or customize the system. Hardware requirements were determined and acquired. These included workstations, server size, scanners, and jukeboxes; along with them came decisions about how much horsepower was needed and what settings and configurations would be used. The software was installed, tested, debugged, and retested. Customizations were implemented. Then, Krom says, PPL tested and tested and tested—and it should have tested more!

The company wisely decided to pilot with a small number of invoices, using one of its smaller affiliate companies first. PPL continued debugging and adjusting the process and software based on feedback from the pilot. It went into full production on January 10, 2000.

LESSONS LEARNED

Krom says it was more difficult to adjust to imaging than he had expected. PPL experienced much resistance from its staff. However, most of these staffers came around fast after using the new system.

The project was more involved and intrusive than assumed, and what was supposed to have been a turnkey solution did not turn out to be so. Although the original start date was projected for October 1999, it was delayed until January 2000. Such delays are not ideal; however, this project came in remarkably close to deadline.

POSSIBLE DOWNSIDE

These systems are expensive. The imaging and workflow system at PPL cost just under $100,000. This includes software, mods, hardware training, and installation. The annual maintenance fee is $6,500. For a company like PPL, with huge volume (300,000 transactions per year), this is not a significant cost, although those with smaller volumes might look for a lower-priced system.

More of an issue was resistance to the new project. The imaging and workflow resulted in several significant changes in the AP department, and not all of the staff were happy about these revisions.

Scanning is a skill that requires practice. If your company deals with many differently shaped and colored invoices, be prepared not to receive an exact match.

FINAL THOUGHTS

More time and effort were needed up front for document preparation and sorting. Krom had to add a person to handle the increased workload.

PPL, like many other companies, experienced an invoice-processing backlog during the implementation of the imaging program. Krom concludes that, even with all this, "We have already begun to realize many of the benefits and expect that to continue. It was an interesting road but worth the effort."

CASE STUDY

An Accounts Payable Web Site

The Internet is the ideal tool to help harried AP professionals deal more effectively with the challenges they encounter. At a recent Accounts Payable conference, Intel's AP controller, Jeff Lupinacci, explained to attendees how his department uses the Internet and offered guidelines on how AP managers could do it themselves.

Do not assume that this was some big fancy project that only an AP department in a *Fortune* 500 company like Intel could pull off. Lupinacci did not use high-powered consultants but rather AP staffers. The entire project cost under $10,000, and that was three years ago. Today, it might be less.

SETTING OBJECTIVES

The most important step in setting up an AP Web site is to determine your objectives. What do you hope to accomplish with the site? Lupinacci determined that Intel needed better customer service for both his internal and external customers, and set out to solve the following problems with the Web site:

- *Reduce phone calls.* The department received a large number of phone calls from both employees and suppliers.
- *Educate client base.* A search was on for a better form of marketing and educating his client base as to AP requirements.
- *Get feedback.* A method for continuous feedback from customers was needed.
- *Reduce costs.* A way to reduce high printing costs of AP forms and an easy way to distribute them was needed.

- *Centralize access.* For pertinent information to be distributed to those who worked outside the AP department, centralized access was needed.

IDENTIFYING RESOURCES AND CONTENT

Getting information technology (IT) resources allocated to any department can be a problem, but an AP department wanting to build its own Web site would perhaps face more obstacles—especially three years ago when both internal and external sites were more novel. Undeterred, the folks at Intel charged ahead. Lupinacci was also lucky. The site for employees was ultimately put up on an intranet (a closed Internet site for company employees only). For this purpose, the company's local area network (LAN) was used to host the site. A personal computer served as the Web server.

Lupinacci pulled together a team of three people who worked on this project for a four-month period. Getting Web content just right is extremely important. Intel spent two months identifying the right content for its AP Web site. Content/process experts were used to validate the information.

DESIGNING THE SITE

If it is not easy to find information on a site, many people will not use it. Recognizing this fact, Intel spent a good deal of time making sure the data was logically arranged. This meant creating a design "bible" before the programming began. It was critical that all information be clear. Lupinacci says that at Intel, roughly a month was spent getting the information arranged and making it logically navigable. He says that they went through many revisions and looks before agreeing on the current design.

To ensure that the site was easily navigable, the amount of animation and pictures was limited. The group identified the appropriate color palette and other visual branding. It was also decided what bells and whistles were needed. Finally, the visual identity created for AP was used on all subsequent marketing efforts.

PULLING THE CONTENT TOGETHER

As the group reached the point where the content solidified, it began converting the files and graphics into formats used on the Web. They chose Anawave's Hotdog Pro and used very few graphics because of system demands. While graphics make a site visually pleasing and entertaining, they also impede the speed at which the site loads.

The formatting was tough because sites can sometimes appear one way on one computer using one browser and another on a different computer. The group had to find a format that looked good on multiple configurations. It is important that those developing their own sites take this into consideration and test their new site on more than one computer. If possible, test its use on an IBM clone and an Apple and, of course, Microsoft Explorer as well as Netscape Navigator.

Keep in mind that from time to time it will be necessary to create new content. Make allowances for this and plan for it in your budget process. Also, allocate the staff time to take care of this chore.

TESTING THE SITE

Quality control is another issue. Lupinacci emphasizes the importance of proofreading the site. It is very easy for spelling errors to creep into the copy. It is also important to have hardware that can withstand the number of visitors you will have to the site. He recommends spending at least two weeks testing and checking the quality of the site; he strongly suggests not launching the site too early. Tell only a few loyal users and let them play around with it until you are sure the kinks have been worked out.

When Intel's AP department first launched its Web site, access was limited within the department. Feedback was obtained via survey and e-mail, with Lupinacci providing incentive for everyone to check it out. The test phase lasted three weeks, with more than 100 people providing input.

MARKETING YOUR ACCOUNTS PAYABLE HOME PAGE

You may think that once you have finally gotten your home page up and running, the battle is over. However, it has just begun. The first step is to make others aware of your Web site. Moving forward, all business documents should have the Web address or uniform resource locator (URL) on them. Intel had a mass mailing to inform employees of the home page. This was sent not only through the internal mail but also via e-mail. In eight months, Lupinacci was able to establish a 79 percent awareness level within the company.

Posters announcing the site were placed in the cafeterias, and an article was published in the in-house IT publication. Organizations with company newsletters can have announcements carried there as well. At Intel, whenever employees called the AP department with a question that could have been answered if they had accessed the Web site, they were pointed in that direction.

Those who develop such a site need to recognize that they will never get 100 percent of potential users to surf for answers. Still, the thought of eliminating more than half the calls coming into AP should provide enough incentive.

MAINTENANCE

A good Web site must be updated frequently, says Lupinacci. He is not alone in this view. If it is not continually fed new information, visitors will not come back to see it again. He recommends continually checking for accuracy, especially if the organization is in a continuous improvement mode. As the company changes its AP policies or procedures, the Web site will have to be updated to reflect these.

Many Web sites have a "What's New" section (or page) that is updated daily, weekly, or monthly—whatever is appropriate for the business. At Intel, the AP "What's New" page is updated every two weeks.

Lupinacci suggests creating links with key business partners as they get their home pages up and running. He gives the example of Finance Information Systems, Purchasing, and Corporate Travel. The links you choose will depend on the nature of the business and whether other departments within the company have their own sites. He reviews the site monthly to ensure data accuracy.

Expect to receive e-mail requests from your Web page. At Intel, the customer service center was established as a mechanism to reply to e-mail. In addition, one full-time employee maintains and updates the AP site. The amount of resources needed to allocate to the site depends on the complexity of the site and the amount of new data added.

He noted that it is important to monitor hardware. What is adequate today may not do the job a year or two down the road.

POST-IMPLEMENTATION

With the site up and running, the amount of user feedback diminishes greatly, but not completely. There needs to be a "gatekeeper," someone responsible for a centralized review of the content, target audience, and placement of the material on the site. Responsibility for content must be assigned so that appropriate information is supplied for updates and improvements. Lupinacci recommends that content be reviewed quarterly and outdated material removed.

Once the site is out there, make sure that it is visited and the right visitors are visiting the right pages. No AP site needs a bunch of teenagers peering through its contents. Hit counters are not enough, says Lupinacci. He wants to know who hits what pages and how long they stay there. This is the information he feels he needs to keep the site top notch.

He captures customer feedback via e-mail. He also surveys his customers annually and at point of service. As an added feature, he involves select customers to participate in usability testing.

Even this is not enough for Lupinacci. Although he benchmarks internally with other functional groups, he continually surfs the Net looking for ideas and standards. However, he says that it is still hard to find other AP sites, although there are a few. He is right. AP is only starting to get the recognition it deserves and, with it, the resources to accomplish what Lupinacci has.

CASE STUDY

How the Accounts Payable Manager at Merck Overhauled Department Procedures and Technology

People, process, and technology were the three keys to AP transformation at Merck, a large company that had been using the same process and technology since 1983. Jim Hinrichs found himself facing this situation in 2000 when he was selected to head Merck's AP group. Speaking at a recent Accounts Payable conference, he explained to attendees the problems the department had when he took over and the techniques he used to address those issues.

BACKGROUND

The Merck AP department was badly in need of an overhaul. In addition to the aforementioned ancient technology, the department had a morale problem coupled with a horrendous absenteeism rate. The staff of 45 turned in an average of 120 sick days each month.

The process had evolved into 90 different business rules and was run more or less as an assembly line. The process was efficient in that an incredible number of payments (2.5 million invoices annually) were pushed through, but accuracy suffered. There were 25,000 active vendors, of which 5 were on electronic data interchange (EDI) and 170 were on electronic funds transfer (EFT).

The system in use was built on a paper-based signature approval process. As you might guess, Merck missed most of its early payment discounts.

Meanwhile, Hinrichs, who had been employed by Merck since 1990, had left in 1997 to take a job as chief financial officer (CFO) of a West Coast technology firm. When he needed to return to the East Coast, he called Merck's CFO to see if there was a place for him at Merck. He returned to head AP and its huge transformation project.

GOALS

In 2000, when Hinrichs took over the renovation of AP—a project referred to as the AP Migration Project—the company had seven goals for the undertaking. Specifically, it wanted to

1. Attack the morale and attendance problems.
2. Automate the U.S. payment process as much as possible.

3. Reduce non–value-added work and manual hand-offs—there was too much paper.

4. Improve customer service to internal customers.

5. Reduce the controllable payment cycle payment time (approval time) from 32 days to 6 days.

6. Make use of new technology to migrate to Merck's accounting system, JD Edwards, and make it work.

7. Use the Intranet to automate as much as possible.

Missed early payment discounts were a sore point at Merck. In 2001, the company spent $7 billion but got only $600,000 in early payment discounts. Clearly, there was room for improvement. When it benchmarked itself against a company that was good at getting these discounts, it was not pleased. McKesson had an annual spend that was slightly more than half of Merck's but had earned $60 million in discounts—almost 100 times better than the Merck performance.

By addressing the three core issues of people, process, and technology, Merck began the transformation of its AP function.

WHAT THEY DID

People

Hinrichs indicated that improving morale hinged on addressing some ugly personnel situations. He says that it was probably the most important step the company took in addressing its AP issues. It began by identifying three individuals who were either not performing or were a menace to the department. Although it was harsh, the goal was to remove these individuals. Two were let go, and the third—either as a fluke or sensing what was to come—left. Hinrichs then took some simple steps that can be emulated by many AP departments. Specifically, he

- Instituted a four-and-a-half-day workweek by having those interested in this schedule work an extra hour each day
- Implemented flextime, which not only gave the employees some breathing room, but gave the department coverage over a longer time period each day
- Set up a change team to address workplace issues such as a nonworking microwave, an uncomfortable sofa in the ladies room, and so on. Although these issues may seem trivial, dealing with them shows the employees that management does care and helps to improve morale.
- Measured morale results by taking an annual employee survey
- Improved attendance. Hinrichs bought a roll of raffle tickets. Each Friday, he gave one to each employee who had not missed a day of work during the week. At the end of the month, he held a drawing for a 27-inch TV. Those who had not missed a day all month had four tickets, those who had missed one day had three entries,and so on. The first month he did this, absenteeism dropped from 120 days to 6 days. It has now leveled off to between 30 and 40 days. Since giving away a TV each month would lose its effectiveness, he now gives $300 to $500 gift certificates at various stores every three months. At first glance, this program may seem expensive. However, he has calculated that he's spent roughly $4,000 since beginning the program and saved the company $140,000 in productivity improvements.
- Reorganized the group into divisional work teams of four to eight people who process invoices for an entire division. The processors became familiar with the vendors and people in the division, and customer service is starting to improve. The few chores that it didn't make

sense to break up, such as mailroom and imaging, remain centralized.

- Hired a manager who focuses continually on process improvements

Process

With 90 different sets of rules, Hinrichs set out to simplify the process as much as possible. He began by splitting invoices into three separate groups:

1. *Purchase order invoices for direct materials.* For Merck, it is crucial that these invoices be handled in as accurate a manner as possible. He noted that in the past the error rate on these items was in the neighborhood of 80 percent, which was not tolerable. The company receives approximately 7,000 invoices of this type each year, and they get special treatment. Messing up on one of these invoices could result in the company's being put on credit hold by a supplier of a crucial component of one of its products, thus halting production. The invoice and receiver are pulled up on the system, and the processor manual matches them online with the purchase order (PO). If everything is okay, a simple click sends the invoice on its way.

2. *PO purchases for nonproduction purchases, by far the largest number of invoices (between 800 and 900,000).* Merck uses the Ariba system for this type of purchase and gets the PO from the Ariba system. The dollar amount of the order determines what type of approval will be needed. If it is less than $5,000, a two-way match is done, and if there is no discrepancy, the invoice is paid. If the invoice is between $5,000 and $15,000, the match is done and an e-mail is sent to the action alert box of the person who ordered the

item, asking for a negative action. The invoice will be paid unless the individual indicates otherwise. If the invoice is over $15,000, a proactive approval is required in order to get the invoice paid. The company uses an e-invoice dispute resolution mechanism. If the invoice does not match the PO, a message is sent to Procurement telling them about the mismatch. Procurement then is required to resolve the dispute before payment can be made.

3. *Those dreaded invoices without POs are automated as much as possible.* They must be approved. Vendors are directed to send invoices to AP. The invoice must include the name of the person who ordered the item, along with the individual's ID number. This is logged into the system with a payment status of "hold." The system then sends an electronic message to the appropriate action alert inbox. The system also checks to see if the person has the authority to approve the dollar amount on the invoice. If not, it sends a similar message to the person's boss, "walking" up the organization chart until it gets to the person at the appropriate approval level.

Hinrichs says that the system is quite flexible and will support current processes, if that is required. He makes the flexibility component clear to all end users. The company learned the hard way when it installed a new T&E system that it couldn't jam new systems down everyone's throats.

Technology

Implementing JD Edwards in AP was probably the most important part of the process to the AP folks, despite meaning nothing to those outside the department. Crucial to the process are the electronic approval requests sent to purchasers. The ability to click on links to see invoices and information helps. If the invoice has an associated PO, the accounting information is prepopulated. The accounting data can be overridden, although the system will check to ensure that a valid account number has been entered.

Hinrichs noted that the ability to click on a button and see the actual invoice has been helpful with those employees who have a dependence on paper. If the invoice involved does not have a PO, the approver must input the account number. The approver can

- Add comments (especially useful if the invoice will be passed up the chain)
- Reject, although a reason must be given
- Delay, although a comment must be added if a discount is involved (He noted that it is not possible to delay indefinitely.)

TRAINING

Clearly, no system such as the one being planned at Merck could go live without education. Hinrichs has put information on the Web site and announcements in the company newsletter and given demos in many departments. He recommends that those involved in projects such as this focus on the high-level administrative assistants, because, he says, in reality they are the ones who will do most of the work—and will eventually train their bosses.

TECHNOLOGY INNOVATIONS ALREADY IMPLEMENTED

Merck planned to go live with its full system several weeks after Hinrichs's talk. The go-live date initially had been scheduled for several weeks before the conference but got pushed back as these things generally do. However, he was able to report on a number of successes, including

- The digital imaging of invoices had already been completed and employees could view any invoice from their home page on the corporate intranet site.
- Employees could also query for invoice status from their home pages. This reduced the number of phone calls coming into AP.
- A Web site was created where vendors can enter invoice information or upload invoices on a simple spreadsheet or something more complicated.
- Use A/Pex Analytics software to catch duplicate payments. How effective is this software? Merck uses a postaudit firm and on $8 billion of spending, it identified $2 million that got by and recovered it all. For those who might be tempted to think this is a large sum, consider that it is significantly less than one tenth of 1 percent.

ACHIEVEMENTS TO DATE

Keeping in mind that the system hasn't gone live fully, the AP department at Merck has made significant inroads. They've spent $11 million and so far have reduced costs $3.3 million and avoided spending another $900,000.

Morale in the department is up as measured by the annual surveys. Absenteeism is down to approximately one third of the old rate. The number of business rules used to process payments has dropped to 30 from 90. The number of EDI vendors has increased from 5 to 12, and the old mainframe has been replaced, as has the old microfilm system. Additionally, the number of EFT vendors has risen from 170 to 1,200. Best of all, 550 vendors are currently using Web invoicing, and the company is adding to that roster at the rate of 200 each month.

This is a big improvement over where the AP department was two years ago. The big payoff will come with the implementation of the new system and the reduction of the controllable payment cycle. This is the time it takes to get approvals on invoices. The big savings will come when Merck qualifies for most, if not all, of the early payment discounts available to it.

IBM's Lou Gerstner's recent book is titled *Who Says Elephants Can't Dance?* Hinrichs has demonstrated that enormous organizations, be they computer companies or pharmaceuticals, can dance quite elegantly if they have the right instructor.

10

Communications/Customer Relations

Often overlooked when discussing accounts payable (AP) are the communications and customer service aspects of the job. If these features are not handled correctly, or not addressed at all, even the most effective AP departments will not be as efficient as they could be. In this chapter, we look at

- Payment status information for vendors
- Communicating relevant information to vendors
- Communicating with internal customers
- Improving the procure-to-pay cycle

PAYMENT STATUS INFORMATION FOR VENDORS

Background

Most vendors are pretty reasonable when it comes to their dealings with AP. They'd like to be paid in full and on time. And they'd like to know the status of their invoices and payments at all times. It helps them resolve discrepancies before the due date, and it helps with their cash forecasting. AP has no control or influence over whether an invoice is paid in full; they simply pay the amount approved by purchasing. They would also like to get fewer of those "Where's my money?" phone calls. It is disruptive to the AP operations to have to constantly stop and research invoice and payment information. So, helping the vendor in this regard also helps AP.

Best Practices

Introduce the concept of self-service to the invoice and payment process. This can be done either on the Web or over the phone through an interactive voice response (IVR) unit. Both of these processes are password protected, so only those who are entitled to the information can get it. Typically, they are based on the invoice number and a company code. The best systems include not only the anticipated payment date but also where the invoice is in the process.

Thus, vendors can check the status as often as they like and then take appropriate action if the invoice isn't where it should be. For example, if the invoice does not appear on the system, the vendor can contact purchasing and send a replacement invoice if it has not been received. The beauty, at least for AP, is that with the vendor eyeing everything, Purchasing can no longer pass the buck to cover for its own shortcomings—if it had that propensity in the past.

The very best of these systems on the Internet also have dispute resolution modules built in. Again, this keeps AP out of the messy process of sorting out disputes that it has no information about. Vendors find these dispute resolution mechanisms attractive, as they allow them to

- Resolve discrepancies/disputes before payment dates
- Get paid on time, as some customers wait until the pay-

ment date to let vendors know of disputes and begin the resolution

- Improve their cash forecasting

Almost Best Practices

If the technology for self-service is not available, assign one or more associates to the customer service function. This individual(s) can answer the inquiries and do the necessary research to provide the vendors the information they require. Those who segregate this function find that the rest of the AP staff appreciates not having to continually respond to these inquiries. However, sometimes staffing the customer response positions can be difficult, as it is a unique individual who likes this type of position.

Reality Check for Accounts Payable

If it is difficult to find an associate to staff the customer service hotline, try rotating the position for a month or two. While this might not provide the continuity desired, it does get the staff cross-trained in a vital position.

Worst Practices

Worst practices include having no specialized customer service function in the AP department. It is inefficient to have every associate answering queries.

COMMUNICATING RELEVANT INFORMATION TO VENDORS

Background

Although payment and invoice status information is important to vendors, it is not the only information needed by vendors. If the vendors are not educated in the beginning about what they need to do to get paid, the payment process is likely to be rocky—especially from the vendors' point of view. Similarly, when a payment is sent, if it is not for the exact amount of the invoice, the vendor is likely to have questions. And those questions will result in numerous phone calls to AP. This leads to poor vendor relations and inefficiencies in the AP department. Hence, anything that can be done to improve the information flow to vendors not only improves vendor relations, but also the efficiency of the department.

Best Practices

From the start, vendors should have all the information they need about your processes, procedures, and requirements. This can be done utilizing one or more of the following vehicles:

- A welcome letter spelling out your requirements, such as
  - Where invoice should be sent
  - Special terms
  - Bill-To address
  - Other special requirements
- A handbook specifying requirements for payment. This can be quite detailed, as is the case with some of the bigger retailers.
- A spot on the Web site that spells out the information that is included in the manual or in the welcome letter. This allows the vendor to know what it is getting into before the fact.

Vendors also require the following information for AP contacts:

- Names

- Phone numbers
- E-mail addresses

While this may seem obvious, it is one of the issues that vendors repeatedly bring up when asked about discussing relations with their customers. Needless to say, this information should be updated and shared with vendors whenever there is a change. Posting it on the Web site is also a good idea.

Letting the vendor know what is expected is only the first step. As discussed here, providing a self-service function that allows vendors to check on payment and invoice status is another best practice, especially if dispute resolution can be incorporated.

The other area that can be improved relatively easily is the sharing of information with vendors when anything other than the full amount is paid on an invoice. Make no mistake about it, sharing the information will not end the phone calls, but it will reduce the number of phone calls needed to resolve issues. Most deductions taken by companies will fall into several broad categories. Although some of the deductions, such as early payment discounts, damaged goods, short shipments, and penalties, might be commonplace, others will be unique to the company or industry. Prepare a simple form that can be included with the payment. The user can simply check off the appropriate boxes and/or add a few words that let the vendor know the reason for the deduction. This information can be included in a paper form or sent by e-mail. When the vendor receives the data, it may still call. However, the call asking the reason for the deduction and the ensuing research will be eliminated.

Almost Best Practices

If the company prefers not to share this information, the AP staff should make some simple notes detailing the reasons for the deductions. Then, when the inevitable phone calls do come, the staff can refer to the notes and at least get the discussion going in the right direction. Given the nature of technology today, this data should be kept in a shared database, so everyone has access to it and can respond to calls on a timely basis.

Reality Check for Accounts Payable

Calls about payments from vendors will continue regardless of what best practices are instituted by AP. However, the number of phone calls can be reduced greatly by some of these customer service initiatives. If, for example, the payment status information is available on the Internet, take the time to walk the vendor through checking it when they call. Yes, it is quicker to check it yourself. However, the time spent walking the vendor through the process is a good investment, as this vendor will not need to call again.

Worst Practices

Some companies don't share information about deductions with vendors, hoping that the amounts will be so small that the vendor won't call. Sometimes they are correct. But more often than not, the vendor will call numerous times until the issue is resolved. This also leads to frayed vendor relations and could ultimately result in higher prices or a key supplier's deciding not to bid when a request for proposal (RFP) goes out.

COMMUNICATING WITH INTERNAL CUSTOMERS

Background

Companies in which the AP department has a poor image and poor relations with other departments can trace the roots of the problem back to the fact that no one really knows what AP needs in order to get payments made, as well as key cutoff dates.

Best Practices

Accounts Payable needs to communicate its requirements to others in the company. This can be done by

- Sharing the AP policy and procedures manual
- Periodically sending around a short informative AP newsletter
- Publishing the names and contact information of the staffers in AP
- Publishing the cutoff dates for travel and entertainment (T&E) payments and vendor payments

The AP department should have a few pages on the company's Internet or intranet site. The information indicated here should be included on it for all to see. Transparency should be the name of the game. If the AP policy and procedures manual is long—and many are—a shorter synopsis can be included on the Web site and/or in a memo to the rest of the company. It is unrealistic to expect others to wade through it to find the information they need.

Larger companies might want to assign one or more people to a customer service function and answer questions the rest of the company might have with AP-related issues.

As discussed in other parts of this book, the policy and procedures manual should be updated periodically. Perhaps input from other affected areas could be sought the next time the update is done. Those who have input are more likely to conform to the policy than those who don't.

The old adage of walking a mile in someone else's shoes is a good one for AP and other departments. Occasionally, Purchasing and AP are at odds. Having representatives from each department work for a day or two in the other department can lead to a greater understanding of the other's problems. This is also a good idea since the two need to work closely.

Accounts Payable should track errors to find the root cause of problems. With this data, they can identify weak points as well as other departments that may be causing problems. This does not have to be a negative. Let's say that with the error information, it becomes apparent that one purchasing agent is responsible for numerous voided checks. By meeting that agent and reviewing the process, not only can the situation be rectified, but the relationship may also be strengthened.

Whenever a new system is rolled out, representatives from AP should be sent to interact with other departments to ensure that everyone knows how to use it properly.

Finally, AP often has the information that Purchasing can use to negotiate better rates. By working with Purchasing, AP can give Purchasing the information it needs to be more successful.

Almost Best Practices

Send the staff to customer service courses to help them deal with difficult situations.

Reality Check for Accounts Payable

The very nature of the tasks handled in AP make it likely that there will be conflicts from time to time. These conflicts can involve other departments as well as vendors. The goal should be to handle these sticky situations with finesse and tact. Vendors will sometimes try and get AP to pay them earlier than their contracts stipulate; other employees will occasionally blame AP for late payments they caused; and employees who are tardy with their T&E reports will then try and hurry the process when their credit card bills show up.

Worst Practices

Worst practices include

- Ignoring the customer service implications of the AP function
- Not working to share information about AP issues with the rest of the company
- Not working with Purchasing

IMPROVING THE PROCURE-TO-PAY CYCLE

Background

Traditionally, the Purchasing and AP functions were distinct and separate. And, for the time being, that is how they are structured at most companies. However, several factors are now affecting the way corporations look at the whole process. Specifically:

- Online purchasing and use of e-catalogs for employee purchasing
- The way companies continue to streamline processes, sometimes integrating related functions for increased efficiencies
- The joining of Purchasing and AP into one department at some companies
- Purchasing's need for information held in AP systems

Best Practices

Recognize that as the corporate landscape changes, Purchasing and AP will be required to work more closely. A small percentage of companies will have the two groups report to the same manager. Even if that is not the case in your organization, the two will need to work closely to improve the procure-to-pay (P2P) cycle.

As companies move to an electronic purchasing process, the integration of electronic invoicing (e-invoicing) and an electronic payment process will allow companies to realize the greatest cost savings.

The sharing of information about special deals, primarily on the purchase order (PO), will help companies recognize the maximum cost savings and efficiencies between the two groups.

Several AP departments have improved their P2P process by placing a Purchasing executive on the AP staff and vice versa. In these situations, the new employee brings valuable information about "the other side" that allows them to design solutions that work for both sides.

Almost Best Practices

When a new project presents itself, have representatives from both functions design the solution. Not only will the company get a resolution that works for both departments, but the relations between the two groups will improve.

Establish a task force to improve the P2P cycle. Representatives from both the Purchasing and AP departments should work on the project.

Reality Check for Accounts Payable

Just as AP has a long list of actions that Purchasing could take to make the AP function run a little smoother, the Purchasing department has a similar list. In some cases, it is simply that one group doesn't completely understand the requirements of the other, but in others, the list contains some good ideas. Having a fresh set of eyes review the process is always a good idea. Find ways to work with Purchasing, and both groups will benefit.

Worst Practices

Worst practices include allowing Purchasing and AP to operate in silos with little or no integration. The two departments need to communicate on a regular basis. If they don't, companies will miss some really easy opportunities to improve the P2P system—and save money and reduce costs in the process.

CASE STUDY

Interactive Voice Response Frees
Accounts Payable from Annoying
"Where's My Money?" Calls

AP groups being inundated with phone calls regarding payment status will find IVR systems to be a big help. This was especially true at Hoffman-LaRoche, Inc., where the AP staff had two groups of difficult people—suppliers and their own sales force—demanding to know where their payments were. Speaking at a recent conference, Nancy Sampson shared her experiences with IVRs, showing not only the benefits but also what should be expected of an IVR system if a company installs one.

DEFINITION

What is IVR? Interactive voice response systems allow people to interact with computers through their telephones. In the Hoffman-LaRoche example, a caller can obtain information pertaining to the expected payment date of certain invoices by entering a series of numbers in response to prerecorded questions.

BACKGROUND

In 1995, Hoffman-LaRoche, Inc., installed its first IVR unit in the AP department. This was a boon to staff productivity. Suppliers could determine when their payments would be made, and so could the sales staff. This is particularly important at a pharmaceutical company such as Hoffman-LaRoche, because it provides many honoraria to doctors and hospitals. When the salespeople called on one of these people, they wanted to be able to tell that customer when the honorarium money would arrive.

In 1999, the company installed SAP; the existing IVR system was not compatible with SAP and thus was disconnected. Recognizing that this would put a strain on the AP department, the system was replaced by a person to answer questions formerly addressed by the system. This seemed like a reasonable solution. Unfortunately, the vendors and salespeople started calling individual processors, disrupting the workflow of the entire department. Therefore, an SAP-compatible IVR system was quickly purchased.

OVERALL OBJECTIVES

Like many other companies, Hoffman-LaRoche wanted to improve productivity in its AP department. It wanted to

- Use technology to reduce costs
- Reduce non–value-added work
- Maximize the use of employee time
- Increase the level of customer service
- Provide 24/7 service availability

SYSTEM SELECTION

The company reviewed three systems, using three criteria to justify the ultimate selection: cost, efficiency, and compatibility with SAP. The system selected was SAP certified and had one other big advantage: It had already been installed in the Human Resources department. Thus, there were cost savings from the sharing of hardware and piggybacking on already-installed software. Finally, the AP department was able to leverage other in-house resources.

The systems evaluated were Edify Electronic Workforce, Syntellect, and CCS.

SYSTEM REQUIREMENTS

Sampson demanded certain features from the new system. She required that it

- Be simple to use
- Have the ability to transfer to a customer service representative
- Allow a letter to be input with three keystrokes
- Be able to expand beyond the current eight lines currently in use
- Have reports available to measure productivity

She was adamant that the ability to transfer to a live person be part of the system, but that this feature not be available at the beginning of the call. The reports feature measured who was hanging up, what questions the suppliers were asking, and the length of time the calls were taking.

WHAT THE SYSTEM DOES FOR SUPPLIERS

A few conference attendees expressed concern about security issues. Sampson assured the group that unless the persons requesting the information regarding payment had the necessary input information, they would not be able to access the data stored on the IVR system. Specifically, suppliers are able to query the system by

- PO and invoice number
- Invoice number and invoice amount
- Vendor number and invoice number
- Vendor number and invoice amount
- Check number

Only those who are entitled to receive information have the necessary numbers to access the system.

WHAT THE SYSTEM DOES FOR EMPLOYEES

The company's sales reps use IVR to inquire about promotional expense reimbursements and the aforementioned honoraria. These reimbursements go directly to the sales reps or to third parties for expenses relating to sales promotions.

Once the system was up and running, it was discovered that employees were using IVR to inquire about their T&Es and payroll. These calls are routed to a T&E inquiry group or payroll, as appropriate. Sampson hopes to expand the system in the future to include online capabilities over the Internet.

CASE STUDY

How Automated Accounts Payable and Purchasing Systems Mesh at BNSF

When AP and Purchasing departments work closely together, everybody wins. Not only are there fewer internal problems, but the payment process is much smoother—a real benefit to AP. As companies take advantage of new electronic initiatives, the opportunities for the two departments to integrate are more pronounced. This was definitely the case at Burlington Northern Santa Fe Railway (BNSF), a *Fortune* 200 company that operates a railway network in 28 states and Canada. Speaking at a recent conference, two representatives from the company explained how better contracts at their company led to easier payments.

BACKGROUND

At BNSF, AP and sourcing are two separate areas. The two business areas initiated two separate projects, which were separately justified. The AP group, looking to improve its invoice handling, developed FastTrack eAP. Simultaneously, sourcing, looking to improve the way its service contracts were handled, initiated a project called ContractSource.

The two company representatives, Leigh Ann Vernon, general director of e-commerce and strategic sourcing support, and Brian Ammon, director of technology management for corporate accounting, explained that, although the two projects were separately justified, integration of the two was planned from the beginning.

INVOICE MANAGEMENT

Getting Started

Of course, the first issue to be addressed was the rationale for automating the invoice-management function. The speakers explained there were numerous reasons, including to

- Streamline operations
- Reduce manual processes
- Reduce clerical staff requirements

- Provide timely and accurate payments to vendors
- Improve audit controls and compliance
- Engage small and midsize suppliers in an efficient and effective supply chain
- Be part of the overall supply chain management

Utilizing FastTrack eAP, the new automated invoice-management system, presented numerous challenges for the department. For starters, the move from a manual process to an automated one required a huge paradigm shift. The new system had to be integrated with legacy systems, which, as those reading this are all too painfully aware, is never easy.

Initial vendor adoption of a new approach is always touchy, and this situation was no different. The group also had to make vendors comfortable with the approach.

The shift also required that a clear definition of hierarchy for the entire organization be established. This had to be documented and programmed as part of the system so that approvals could be handled in a consistent and accurate manner. There would be no more relying on the AP associate to remember who could approve what.

A cross-functional implementation team was set up. Vendors were involved from the beginning, because their input was crucial so the team did not develop something that was unusable. The project was piloted with a manageable group. Finally, the team was determined to avoid product customizations wherever possible. As anyone who has ever customized software knows, upgrades can be a real problem once a company tinkers with the basic product.

Derived Benefits

As might be expected, the benefits on the staffing side were immediate. There was a reduction in manual processes and clerical positions. The vendors liked the online invoice entry because it was accessible 24/7. They liked the e-mail notification of invoice status and the ability to preview newly created contracts.

CONTRACT MANAGEMENT

Getting Started

The purchasing folks also had to define the benefits they expected to achieve with their new automated system. Specifically, they hoped to

- Streamline operations
- Reduce manual processes
- Automate the contract request process
- Reduce clerical staff requirements
- Provide better response and visibility to stakeholders
- Monitor and manage contract compliance and performance
- Regulate templates and standardization
- Improve audit controls and compliance
- Integrate to ensure accurate payments

This too was part of the overall supply chain management strategy. If you go back and look at some of the reasons the invoice project was initiated by AP, you will note that many are similar to those offered by those responsible for contract management.

Contract management faced many challenges, a number quite similar to the ones encountered by their AP peers. They too had to deal with a paradigm shift from manual processes to an automated approach.

Customer acceptance, training, and integration were also issues. A unique challenge was the conversion of existing contracts and templates to the new system, not an easy undertaking under the best of circumstances.

A cross-functional implementation team was selected. The contract template, key to the success of the project, was reviewed. Again, there was a pilot with a manageable area and a few specific contracts. Like their AP peers, the procurement folks avoided product customizations wherever possible and got a few customers involved before the implementation.

Derived Benefits

The company reported that it had its full return on investment (ROI) in 62 days—definitely not a shabby outcome. It also reported a 72 percent reduction in contract management efforts. Like the group in AP, it was almost immediately able to trim its manual processes. The 16-step manual process was reduced to a seven-step automated routine. Thus, there was a decline in the requirements for its clerical staff. Best of all, the new streamlined contract process cycle has gone from 30 days to 11 days!

Everyone is happy with the online contract access and request. As with the prior group, the 24/7 access has been a big hit, as is the e-mail notification of contract status and the ability to preview newly created contracts.

SUCCESS FACTORS

Many reading this will be able to recount horror stories of electronic initiatives that not only did not work but fell flat on their faces. The speakers believe that their success was due to several factors, including sponsorship at senior levels within the company and the fact that a cross-functional team was used to develop the product. By bringing in all the affected areas, everyone's concerns were addressed.

The clear project plan helped a lot, as did the early focus on the end-user and the involvement of those who would ultimately use the system. User training ensured that those who were brought on board stayed there rather than getting discouraged because of an inability to effectively use the system. Finally, the speakers claim they had one other secret to their success: constant communication. As with any other high-visibility project, it was important that everyone be kept in the loop.

WHAT'S NEXT?

Not satisfied to rest on its laurels, the company is looking for ways to improve and expand on its recent accomplishments. It hopes to expand the vendor interface capabilities of its Fast-Track eAP system as well as broaden the use of Contract-Source to other units within the company. It also plans on rolling out RFP functionality for its contract management product.

The two groups continuously look for ways to improve their business processes. One of the ways they do this is to seek customer and user feedback. They also participate in the Upside Software (software used for the products) functional improvement program.

The BNSF program demonstrates what a company with its eyes firmly focused on the future can do. The speakers showed how a company in what many consider a stodgy business can be a real showstopper.

Index

Index

Index

Index

CPSIA information can be obtained at www.ICGtesting.com
264138BV00007B/12/P